An Introduction to Systemic Linguistics

2 Levels and Links

An Introduction to Systemic Linguistics

2 Levels and Links

Margaret Berry

**Lecturer in the Department of English,
University of Nottingham**

ST. MARTIN'S PRESS   New York

Contents

To K.J.B.

Preface

This book is intended for students in English departments of universities and colleges of education. It aims at introducing such students to one kind of linguistics, the kind which is usually known as 'systemic linguistics'. Brief remarks are made at intervals in the book about ways in which this kind of linguistics differs from other kinds.

The book deals in turn with each of the most fundamental concepts of systemic linguistics, giving an explanation of each concept and discussing passages of English in relation to the concept. It is hoped in this way to familiarise students with the basic ideas of systemic linguistics, so that they will be able to read with comparative ease the more advanced books and articles on the subject. Suggestions for further reading are given in the bibliography of each chapter.

The book is divided into two volumes: Volume 1, Structures and Systems; and Volume 2, Levels and Links. Volume 1 dealt with the two most basic categories of grammar, structure and system, and with other related grammatical concepts. Volume 2 deals with the levels of language other than grammar and discusses the relationships which exist between the categories within grammar and the relationships which exist between grammar and the other levels. The most important chapters in the book for an understanding of systemic linguistics are Chapters 8 and 9 of Volume 1 and Chapters 2 and 6 of Volume 2, since these chapters deal with the concepts which most distinguish systemic linguistics from other kinds of linguistics.

Further information on the aims and scope of the book is to be found in Section 2.2 of Volume 1.

I make no claim to originality. The ideas expressed are almost all those of other people, notably Professor J. R. Firth, Professor M. A. K. Halliday and Professor J. McH. Sinclair. I apologise to the original authors of the ideas, if I have in any way misrepresented them in my attempt to make

.ie ideas easily intelligible to people who have little or no prior knowledge of linguistics.

I should like to thank all those who, directly or indirectly, have helped in the writing of the book: Professor M. A. K. Halliday, Professor J. McH. Sinclair and Mr J. G. Williamson who read the first draft and made numerous extremely helpful comments and who have also given a great deal of general help and encouragement; others who read and commented on parts of the first draft, including Dr R. A. Hudson and Dr R. I. Page; students, friends and colleagues at the University of Nottingham 1960-73, discussions with whom have been invaluable, especially Mr D. Evans, Mr C. S. Butler, Mr B. J. Calder, Dr R. G. Keightley, Dr W. Nash, Dr R. R. K. Hartmann and Mr C. J. Pountain; Professor P. Hodgson and Mrs V. G. Salmon of Bedford College, University of London, who first encouraged my interest in linguistics; Professor K. Cameron and Professor J. Kinsley of the University of Nottingham who made it possible for me to follow up this interest; and my mother and father, who have helped by typing the manuscript, drawing diagrams and checking proofs, and whose general encouragement has been even more valuable than their active assistance in the preparation of the book.

In spite of all the assistance which I have received, there still remain many faults in the book. For these I am, of course, solely responsible.

1
Introduction

This chapter summarises the main points made in Volume 1.

1.1 SYSTEMIC LINGUISTICS AND THE SOCIOLOGICAL ASPECTS OF LANGUAGE

Language can be studied from a number of different points of view. Of all the aspects of language which it is possible to consider, systemic linguistics is most concerned with certain of the sociological aspects of language.

When discussing the sociological interests of systemic linguistics, the key words are perhaps *behaviour, function, situation.* Systemic linguistics views language as a form of behaviour, as something that we do. It views language as a form of behaviour which is functional, as something that we do with a purpose, or more often in fact with more than one purpose. It views language as a form of functional behaviour which is related to the social situation in which it occurs, as something that we do purposefully in a particular social setting.

Systemic linguistics is interested in relating the internal organisation of language, the various kinds of patterning which language exhibits, to the functions of language and to the social situations of language. It is interested in showing which bits of which patterns are determined by which functions of language. It is interested in showing how the patterning varies in different social settings.

(For further discussions of the main interests of systemic linguistics see Chapter 2 of Volume 1.)

1.2 LEVELS OF LANGUAGE

To cater for the different kinds of patterning and the various aspects of situation which are to be related to each other, systemic linguistics

postulates a number of *levels* and *interlevels* of language, each with a
number of subdivisions or *sublevels.*

FIGURE 3^1.1*   *The levels of language*

SUBSTANCE	←——→	FORM	←——→	SITUATION
phonic substance graphic substance	phonology graphology	grammar lexis	context	thesis immediate situation wider situation

Systemic linguistics recognises three primary levels of language:
substance, form and *situation.*

Substance is the raw material of language. It can be divided into *phonic
substance,* the sounds we use when we speak, and *graphic substance,* the
symbols we use when we write.

Form is the way in which substance is organised into recognisable bits
of a given language. For instance the bits of graphic substance, *a, a, i, y, p,
l, f, r* can be organised into recognisable bits of English such as *fair play*
or *play fair.* Form is subdivided into *lexis* and *grammar.* Lexis caters for
the kind of patterning which operates between individual linguistic items
such as *play* and *fair.* Grammar caters for the kind of patterning which
operates between types of linguistic item such as verb and noun. The
lexical patterns of *fair play* and *play fair* are alike in that they are composed of the same individual linguistic items. The grammatical patterns of
fair play and *play fair* however are composed of different types of linguistic
item: in the one case adjective + noun, in the other case verb + adverb.

Situation is what it sounds like, the situation in which language is used.
There are many aspects of situation to which we want to relate the sound
patterning, the symbol patterning, the lexical patterning and the grammatical patterning referred to in the last two paragraphs. One way of
subdividing situation so as to show the range of the relevant aspects of
situation is into *thesis, immediate situation* and *wider situation.* The
thesis situation is the situation that the language is about. The immediate
situation is the set of circumstances which actually apply when the language is being used. The wider situation is the set of circumstances which
make up the background of the participants in the immediate situation.
Thus when Eliza in *My Fair Lady* sings *The rain in Spain stays mainly in
the plain,* the thesis situation has to do with the country of Spain, flat
lands, rain and its habits. The immediate situation consists of Eliza per-

---

*A superscript[1] in the number of a diagram indicates that it is repeated from
Volume 1. The rest of the number is the number assigned to it in Volume 1, the
first figure of the number indicating the chapter of Volume 1 in which it occurs.

forming an elocution exercise under the direction of Henry Higgins in
Henry Higgins' house. The wider situation includes Eliza's background
as a cockney flower girl and also Henry Higgins' background and interests.

In addition to the three primary levels with their subdividions, systemic
linguistics recognises interlevels which cater for the relationships between
the primary levels. *Phonology* relates phonic substance to lexis and grammar.
Graphology relates graphic substance to lexis and grammar. *Context*
relates lexis and grammar to thesis, immediate situation and wider situation.

(Further discussion of the levels of language can be found in Chapter
3 of Volume 1.)

1.3   THE AXES OF CHAIN AND CHOICE

Reference has been made in the last two sections to the patterning of
language. Examples provided us with instances of graphological patterning,
$p + l + a + y$ and $f + a + i + r$, instances of lexical patterning, *fair + play*
and *play + fair,* and instances of grammatical patterning, adjective + noun
and verb + adverb. Each of these patterns consists of things occurring
one after another in a line. The dimension along which these patterns
occur is called the *axis of chain* or the *syntagmatic axis.*

At each point in each pattern we make a choice. For instance in the
graphological pattern $f + a + i + r$, f has been chosen rather than p or h. In
the lexical pattern *fair + play, fair* has been chosen rather than *unfair.* In
each case what has been chosen contrasts with what has not been chosen
in such a way as to signal a difference in meaning. The dimension along
which something that has been chosen relates to the things that have not
been chosen, the things with which it contrasts, is called the *axis of
choice* or the *paradigmatic axis.*

The notion of contrasting choices is particularly important in systemic
linguistics and relates to the view of language as behaviour. What we do
seems all the more significant when we consider it in the light of what we
might have done but did not do. The main task of systemic linguistics is
to discover what we 'can do' at each level of language; that is, to discover
what options are possible at each level of language and to show how they
contrast along the axis of choice. Particular instances of language, what
particular people 'do do' with language on particular occasions can then
be considered in the light of what they 'can do'.

Not only does systemic linguistics want to relate phonological, graphological, lexical and grammatical patterns along the axis of chain to

function and situation, as suggested above. It also wants to relate the
contrasting choices at each level to function and situation. It is interested
in showing which choices relate to which functions. It is interested in
showing which options are available in which social settings, which options
are most frequently chosen in which social settings.

(Further discussion of the axes of chain and choice can be found in
Chapter 4 of Volume 1.)

1.4   THE STRUCTURES OF GRAMMAR

So far we have been considering the main interests of systemic linguistics
and the most basic of all concepts of systemic linguistics – the levels of
language and the axes of chain and choice. We now turn more specifically
to the level of grammar. We shall first consider the patterns of the level of
grammar and then later its contrasting choices.

The patterns of grammar are called *structures*. Each structure consists
of *elements*.

The sentences

Ex. 1.1   *Aunt Jemima patted the dog timorously*
Ex. 1.2   *She sells sea-shells on the sea-shore*

exemplify the structure SPCA. Each consists of the element *subject* (S),
the element *predicator* (P), the element *complement* (C), and the element
adjunct (A).

SUBJECT	PREDICATOR	COMPLEMENT	ADJUNCT
Aunt Jemima	*patted*	*the dog*	*timorously*
She	*sells*	*sea-shells*	*on the sea-shore*

The sentences

Ex. 1.3   *Make hay while the sun shines*
Ex. 1.4   *She ran away because she was afraid*

exemplify the structure α β. Each consists of the element *main* (α), and
the element *subordinate* (β).

MAIN	SUBORDINATE
Make hay	*while the sun shines*
She ran away	*because she was afraid*

The underlined stretches of the sentences

Ex. 1.5   *The cottages nearby were very picturesque*
Ex. 1.6   *A stitch in time saves nine*

exemplify the structure m h q. Each consists of the element *modifier* (m), *headword* (h) and *qualifier* (q).

MODIFIER	HEADWORD	QUALIFIER
The	*cottages*	*nearby*
A	*stitch*	*in time*

Each of these structures is an amalgam of a number of other structures, each of which is relatable to one of the main functions of language. For instance Ex. 1.1 can be said to have the structure *actor + action + goal + circumstance.* This is relatable to the function of language to be about something. Ex. 1.1 is about somebody who does something to something in a particular manner. Ex. 1.1. can also be said to have the structure *mood marker[1] + mood marker[2] + support.* This is relatable to the function of language to set up some kind of interaction between speaker and hearer. The kind of interaction set up by Ex. 1.1 is different from the kind of interaction set up by Ex. 1.7 or Ex. 1.8.

Ex. 1.7   *Did Aunt Jemima pat the dog timorously?*
Ex. 1.8   *Aunt Jemima, pat the dog timorously!*

The bits of the sentence which indicate what kind of interaction is being set up are the first two bits, the bits which have been labelled *mood marker[1]* and *mood marker[2]*. Ex. 1.1 can also be said to have the structure *theme + rheme.* This is relatable to the function of language to indicate to the hearer how the various ingredients of a message fit together in the message. The theme is the starting-point of the message; the rheme is what is said about that starting-point. The starting-point, the theme, of Ex. 1.1 is different from the starting-point of Ex. 1.9.

Ex. 1.9   *The dog Aunt Jemima patted timorously (but the cat she stroked with enthusiasm)*

Ex. 1.1	*Aunt Jemima*	*patted*	*the dog*	*timorously*
Elemental structure	S	P	C	A
Functional structures	actor mood marker[1] theme	action mood marker[2] rheme	goal support	circumstance

Each of the first kind of structures discussed in this section, the structures which consist of elements, is the result of the conflation of a number of the second kind of structures, the structures relatable to functions. (The way in which functional structures are conflated to form elemental structures will be indicated in Chapter 2 of this volume.)

The things of which the functional structures are composed are themselves called *functions*. Thus actor, action, goal, circumstance, mood marker[1], mood marker[2], support, theme, rheme are all functions. They are sometimes called *micro-functions* to distinguish them from the main functions or purposes of language, which are sometimes called *macro-functions*. The term *function* will from now on in this book, to avoid confusion, be reserved for the micro-functions. When the main functions of language, the macro-functions, are further discussed in Chapter 6, an alternative term will be used for them, as will be indicated then.

(Further discussion of structures and functions and further examples of structures of English can be found in Chapter 5 of Volume 1.)

1.5   THE UNITS OF GRAMMAR

The stretches of language which carry the structures of grammar differ in their relative sizes. The stretches of language which carry SPCA structures are bigger, relatively speaking, than the stretches of language which carry mhq structures. The stretches of language which carry $\alpha\beta$ structures are bigger, relatively speaking, than the stretches of language which carry SPCA structures. The different sizes of stretch of language are called *units*.

English is usually said to have five basic grammatical units: the *sentence*, the *clause*, the *group*, the *word* and the *morpheme*. The stretches of language which carry $\alpha\beta$ and other similar structures are called *sentences*. The stretches of language which carry SPCA and other similar structures are called clauses. The stretches of language which carry mhq and other similar structures are called *groups*. Words carry structures such as *base* +

ending, as in *paints,* and such as *base + suffix,* as in *painter.* Morphemes, being the smallest grammatical units, do not carry structures of their own. They are the bits that make up the structures of words. Thus *paint, er* and *s* are morphemes.

(Further discussion of units can be found in Chapter 6 of Volume 1.)

1.6 THE RANK SCALE OF GRAMMAR

As implied in Section 1.5, the units can be arranged on a scale according to their size. This scale is called the *rank* scale. The simplest form of the rank scale for the English grammatical units is:

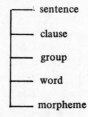

Usually we expect that each unit will be made up of members of the unit next below it on the scale. Thus we should usually expect sentences to be made up of clauses, clauses to be made up of groups, groups to be made up of words, words to be made up of morphemes.

Ex. 1.5 *The cottages nearby were very picturesque*

is one sentence. The sentence consists of one clause. The clause is made up of three groups. The groups consist of three words, one word and two words respectively. The three words of the first group consist of one morpheme, two morphemes and two morphemes respectively. The word of the second group consists of two morphemes (though actually this is debatable). The words of the third group consist of one morpheme and two morphemes respectively.

Ex. 1.5 ||| || *The cottage⁺s near⁺by* | *w⁺ere* | *very pictur⁺esque* || |||

(||| = sentence boundary || = clause boundary
  | = group boundary   + = morpheme boundary)

When we say that each unit will be made up of members of the unit

next below, what we really mean is that each element of a unit's structure
will be represented by a member of the unit next below. Thus we should
usually expect the elements of sentence structure, α and β, to be represented by clauses, the elements of clause structure, S, P, C and A, to be
represented by groups, the elements of group structure, such as m, h and q,
to be represented by words, the elements of word structure, such as base,
suffix and ending to be represented by morphemes. In Ex. 1.5 this is
exactly what happens.

Ex.   1.5

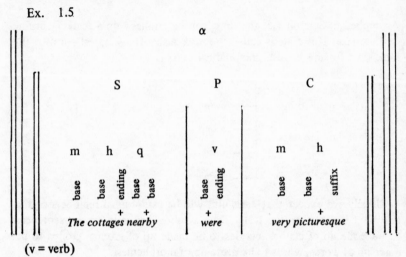

(v = verb)

However sometimes an element of a unit's structure can be represented
by a member of a unit of equal rank or sometimes even by a member of a
unit of higher rank. In Ex. 1.5 the element q of the structure of the first
group is represented as we should expect by a word, *nearby.* But in Ex. 1.10
the element q of the structure of the first group is represented by a
group, *of local stone,* a member of a unit of equal rank. And in Ex. 1.11
the element q of the structure of the first group is represented by a clause,
which were of local stone, a member of a unit of higher rank.

Ex. 1.10   *The cottages of local stone were very picturesque*
Ex. 1.11   *The cottages which were of local stone were very picturesque*

					α			
			S			P	C	
		m	h	q				
Ex. 1.5		The cottages nearby				were	very picturesque	
Ex. 1.10		The cottages [of local stone]				were	very picturesque	
Ex. 1.11		The cottages [[which were of local stone]]				were	very picturesque	

The bracketed group and the bracketed clause are each operating in the same way as the single word *nearby*. When in this way a member of one unit operates in the same way as a member of a lower unit, it is said to have undergone *rankshift*.

([ ] = rankshifted group   [[ ]] = rankshifted clause)

(Further discussion of rank and rankshift can be found in Chapter 7 of Volume 1.)

1.7   THE SYSTEMS OF GRAMMAR

We have now considered the patterns of grammar, the structures, and we have seen that these structures are carried by different ranks of unit. The different ranks of unit also carry contrasting choices. Each rank of unit acts as an *entry condition* which opens the way to a set of *systems,* a system being a set of options available in the grammar of a language.

For instance in English the unit clause acts as entry condition to the *transitivity* systems. Each clause chooses between a number of different types of *process.* For example each clause chooses between *material process* as in

Ex. 1.12   *Keegan kicked the ball to Toshack*

mental process as in

Ex. 1.13   *Theodore saw a curlew on Saturday*

and *relational process* as in

    Ex. 1.14   *John is a teacher*

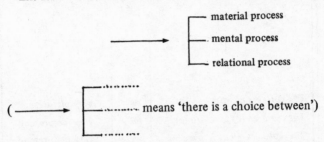

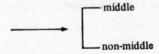
(means 'there is a choice between')

Those clauses which have chosen material process* also make a choice between *middle* process (a process with an actor but no goal) as in

    Ex. 1.15   *John walked slowly*

and *non-middle* process (a process with both actor and goal) as in

    Ex. 1.12   *Keegan kicked the ball to Toshack*

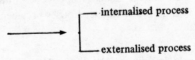

Those clauses which have chosen mental process also make a choice between *internalised process* as in

    Ex. 1.13   *Theodore saw a curlew on Saturday*

and *externalised process* as in

    Ex. 1.16   *John said that yesterday*

                          — internalised process

                          — externalised process

---

*More accurately, those clauses which have chosen material process and restricted process also make a choice between middle and non-middle. See Volume 1 pages 156-7.

Those clauses which have chosen mental process and internalised process also make a choice between *perception process* as in

Ex. 1.13 *Theodore saw a curlew on Saturday*

reaction process as in

Ex. 1.17 *Cats like fish*

and *cognition process* as in

Ex. 1.18 *Aunt Jemima considered her predicament*

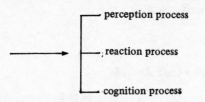

As well as acting as entry condition to the transitivity systems, the unit clause also acts as entry condition to the *theme* systems. For instance each clause chooses between *unmarked theme* (the theme being represented by the same bit of language as mood marker[1]) as in

Ex. 1.1 *Aunt Jemima patted the dog timorously*

and *marked theme* (the theme being represented by a different bit of language from mood marker[1]) as in

Ex. 1.9 *The dog Aunt Jemima patted timorously (but the cat she stroked with enthusiasm)*

As their names suggest unmarked theme is the more usual, marked theme the more unusual of these two options.

A clause which is acting as the α element of a sentence is the entry condition to the *mood* systems. Each α clause chooses between *indicative* as in

Ex. 1.15 *John walked slowly*

and *imperative* as in

Ex. 1.19   *Walk slowly, John*

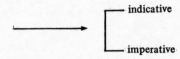

Those α clauses which have chosen indicative also make a choice between *declarative* as in

Ex. 1.15   *John walked slowly*

and *interrogative* as in

Ex. 1.20   *Did John walk slowly?*

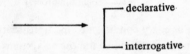

Each of the sets of systems discussed so far, transitivity, theme and mood, is, as will be seen in Chapter 6, relatable to one of the main or macro-functions of language.

Some systems have more than one set of entry conditions. The *number* systems for instance can be entered via the clause or via the group. Each clause chooses between *singular* as in

Ex. 1.21   *Aunt Jemima's cat likes fish*

and *plural* as in

Ex. 1.17   *Cats like fish*

In addition to the choice made by the clause some groups acting as complements and some groups acting as adjuncts can also make choices from number systems. In

Ex. 1.13   *Theodore saw a curlew on Saturday*
Ex. 1.22   *Theodore saw some curlews on Saturday*

each clause as a whole has chosen singular. But the groups acting as their complements differ in their choices from the number systems, that of Ex. 1.13 choosing singular, that of Ex. 1.22 choosing plural.

We have then looked at some examples of English grammatical systems. We must now consider more precisely just what a system is.

We have said that a system is a set of options, a set of contrasting choices. We have implied that it is a set of options available under certain conditions, these conditions being specified partly in terms of the rank of unit to which the system is applicable, partly in terms of the part the unit is playing in the structure of a higher unit, partly in terms of the other options which must be chosen before the options of the given system become available.

We can say further that a system is a set of options with three essential properties.

1. The options in a system, which are known as the *terms* in the system, are mutually exclusive. If an α clause is declarative it cannot at the same time be interrogative. The selection of declarative precludes the selection of interrogative.

2. A system is finite. It is possible to fix a limit for a system and to say that it consists of a certain countable number of terms, no more, no less. The limit is set in such a way that all the terms which are mutually exclusive with each other are included in the system, while any terms not mutually exclusive with those in the system are excluded from the system.

3. The meaning of each term in a system depends on the meaning of the other terms in the system. If the meaning of one of the terms in a system is changed, the meaning of other terms in the system will also change. If a term is added to a system or subtracted from a system, the meaning of the other terms in the system will change. For instance, if we compare the number systems of Old English with the number systems of present-day English we find that where Old English had three terms in one of its number systems, present-day English has only two.

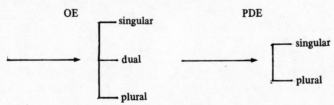

The fact that present-day English has one term fewer gives its plural term a different value from the plural term of Old English. The plural term of

FIGURE 9¹.7

The transitivity and voice network

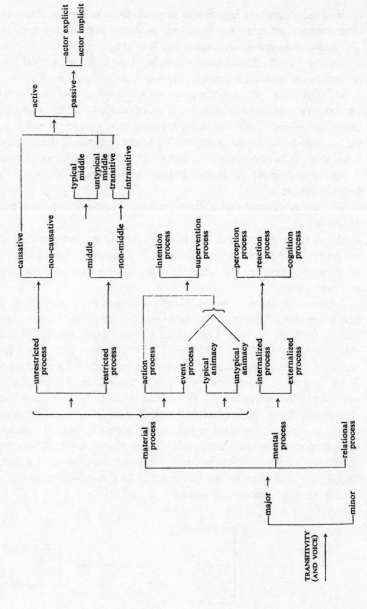

Old English meant 'more than two'; the plural term of present-day English means 'more than one'.

(Further discussion of systems and further examples of the grammatical systems of English can be found in Chapter 8 of Volume 1.)

1.8   THE SCALE OF DELICACY

We have seen that the units of grammar are related on a scale of rank. The systems of grammar are related on a scale of *delicacy*.

Figure 9^1.7 shows how the transitivity systems discussed in Section 1.7 form a *network* together with other transitivity systems and together with some of the *voice* systems such as the choice between *active* and *passive*.

The notation

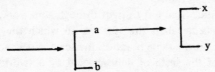

means that the system to the right is dependent on the system to the left; that is, that a choice between the terms of the righthand system is possible only if term a has been chosen from the lefthand system.

The notation

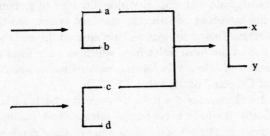

means that a choice between x and y is possible if either term a has been chosen or term c has been chosen.

The notation

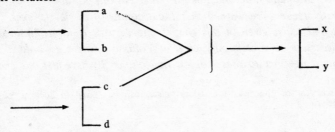

means that a choice between x and y is possible only if both a and c have been chosen.

The notation

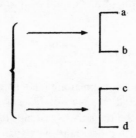

means that the two systems are simultaneous; that is, that they have exactly the same entry conditions.

The scale of delicacy runs from left to right through a network. Systems are said to be more *delicate* than the systems on which they depend. Simultaneous systems are at the same point on the scale of delicacy.

(Further discussion of the scale of delicacy and of networks can be found in Chapter 9 of Volume 1.)

In this chapter then we have considered briefly the main interests of systemic linguistics, the levels of language postulated by systemic linguistics and the axes of chain and choice. Within the level of grammar we have considered the categories of structure, unit and system and the scales of rank and delicacy. This means that we have covered three of the four categories and two of the three scales from which an early form of systemic linguistics, *scale-and-category linguistics,* took its name. The third scale is the subject of Chapter 2 of this volume.*

Chapter 2 will consider the links between the levels of language and more specifically the links between the categories of grammar. The remaining chapters of this volume will consider in more detail each of the levels of language other than grammar, reverting at intervals to the question of the links between the levels.

Two cautionary notes must be introduced at this point.

Firstly readers are warned that the accounts of the levels, axes, categories and scales given in this chapter are very much oversimplified. It was necessary to oversimplify even in Volume 1 where a whole volume was being devoted to these topics. In Volume 2 where just one chapter

*A discussion of the fourth category, *class,* can be found in Section 5.2.3 of Volume 1.

has been devoted to them the accounts are even more oversimplified.

Secondly, as was pointed out in Volume 1, there are disagreements among systemic linguists. Not all systemic linguists would agree with all that has been said in this chapter.

2
Grammar: Realisation

The scale of **realisation** is perhaps the most important scale of all. It shows how the different levels of language are related to each other; and within each level it shows how the different categories, such as structure and system, are related to each other.

2.1 REALISATION RELATIONSHIPS BETWEEN THE LEVELS OF LANGUAGE

A speaker or writer of language wishes to communicate something about some aspect of situation. To do this he makes generalisations about situation or, more usually, he makes use of generalisations which have been made about situation by previous speakers and writers of his language. The generalisations are of two kinds.

One kind of generalisation involves noticing that certain objects or qualities or actions have similar properties and marking the similarity between them by giving them the same name. For example objects with seats, backs and legs of certain proportions are all called, in English, *chairs*.

The second kind of generalisation involves noticing properties of a situation which recur in connection with different objects or qualities or actions and marking the recurrence of each property by a particular feature of language. For example objects or qualities or actions may have the property of singleness or the property of non-singleness. If they have the property of singleness they will, in English, be marked in some way as being singular. If they have the property of non-singleness they will, in English, be marked in some way as being plural.

The processes of generalisation take the speaker or writer from the level of situation into the interlevel of context.

The naming which follows the first kind of generalisation takes the speaker or writer across from the interlevel of context into the formal level of lexis. The relationship between the interlevel of context and the formal level of lexis is a realisation relationship. Each concept which results from the first kind of generalisation **is realised by** a lexical item. The concept of a chair is realised by the lexical item *chair*.

The second kind of generalisation takes the speaker or writer from the interlevel of context into the formal level of grammar. Here again the relationship between the interlevel and the formal level is a realisation relationship. A concept resulting from the second kind of generalisation is realised by a grammatical item or a grammatical pattern. The concept of plural is realised by a morpheme such as *s* which acts as an ending in the structure of a word.

A speaker or writer needs to do more than make, or recall, generalisations and think of the appropriate formal items or patterns. If he is to communicate, he must make the formal items and patterns manifest in some way; he must make them audible or visible. Formal items and patterns need to be realised by phonology or graphology. The lexical item *chair* is realised either by a sequence of letters, *c, h, a, i, r,* or by a corresponding sequence of sounds. The plural morpheme referred to above is realised either by a sequence of letters, such as *s,* or *es,* or by a corresponding sequence of sounds.

Even in the interlevels of phonology and graphology, the speaker or writer has not quite reached the audible or visible manifestation of what he wishes to communicate. The phonological or graphological items need to be realised by phonic or graphic substance. We think of the letter *h* as a single letter and in graphological terms, so it is. But in terms of graphic substance, *h* is only one realisation of a graphological item which can be realised in a number of different ways. *h,* h *,ℎ,* for instance, are alternative realisations of this letter. In *chair,* the shape *h* is realising the letter *h.* In chair , the shape h is realising this letter.

The scale of realisation, as described so far, is shown in Figure 2.1.

Each stage on the realisation scale takes the speaker or writer one degree nearer to the audible or visible manifestation of what he wishes to communicate about situation. The term *is realised by* can in fact be paraphrased as 'is manifested by' or 'is made manifest by', 'is implemented phrases of the term which contribute to an understanding of its meaning are 'is represented by', 'is encoded by', 'is evidenced by', 'is implemented by', 'is expounded by'.

The arrows in the diagram should really be two-directional, as they are in Figure 2.2. The **realises** relationship is important, as well as the 'is realised by' relationship. The direction of the 'is realised by' relationship represents the point of view of a speaker or writer. The direction of the 'realises' relationship represents the point of view of a hearer or reader.

A reader sees a series of shapes, such as *Chairs not to be taken beyond*

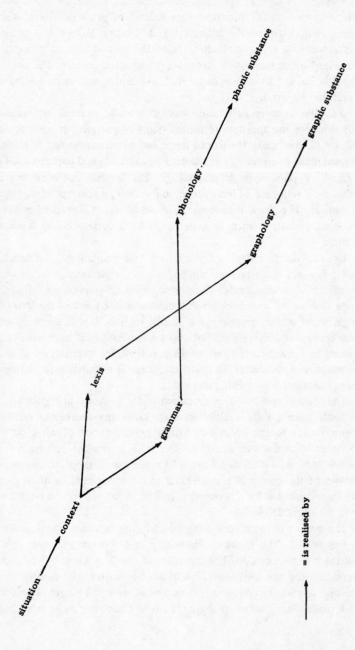

FIGURE 2.1   *The 'is realised by' relationships between the levels of language*

= is realised by

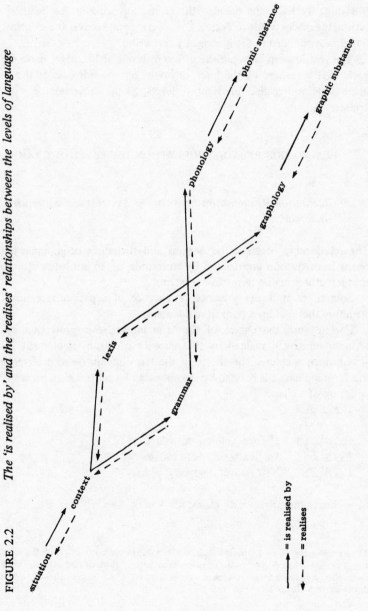

FIGURE 2.2   *The 'is realised by' and the 'realises' relationships between the levels of language*

this point. He knows that each shape, such as *h,* realises a letter, that each letter, such as *s,* or each combination of letters, such as *chair,* realises a grammatical item or a lexical item and that each grammatical or lexical item realises a concept resulting from a generalisation about situation. By following through the realisation scale in the 'realises' direction, the reader is able to decode the message and recover the information which was encoded in the message by the writer.

The relationship between the different levels of language, then, is that each level is realised by the level, or levels, on one side of it on the realisation scale and realises the level, or levels, on the other side of it on the scale.

2.2   REALISATION RELATIONSHIPS WITHIN THE LEVEL OF GRAMMAR

2.2.1   *Realisation Relationships between the Systems and Structures of Grammar*

The relationship between the systems and structures of grammar is that terms from systems are realised by structures, or, to put it the other way, that structures realise terms from systems.

Sometimes it is the presence or absence of a particular element of structure that realises a term from a system.

For instance the choice of the term indicative in preference to the term imperative is realised by the presence of a subject element in the structure of a clause. The choice of the term imperative in preference to the term indicative is realised by the absence of a subject element from the structure of a clause.

The clauses

Ex. 8^1.86*   *Has John closed the door?*
Ex. 8^1.87   *Small boys are naturally dirty*
Ex. 8^1.88   *Well-trained dogs keep to heel*

have chosen indicative. Each clause has a subject element.

---

*The numbering of an example indicates the point in the book at which the example was first introduced, the first figure in each case indicating the relevant chapter. Examples whose chapter references are followed by a superscript [1] were first discussed in Volume 1.

The clauses

Ex. 8^1.90   *Wash behind your ears!*
Ex. 8^1.91   *Keep to heel!*

have chosen imperative. Neither clause has a subject element.

Of course some imperative clauses can be said to have a kind of subject, as for instance

Ex. 8^1.89   *Close the door, Theodore!*
Ex. 2.1   *Theodore, close the door!*

But it is a different kind of subject from the subjects of indicative clauses. The difference is marked in written English by the insertion of a comma and in spoken English by the use of a different stress and intonation pattern, and possibly by a pause between the 'subject' and the rest of the clause. *Close the door, Theodore!* also marks the difference by placing *Theodore* in a different position in the sequence of elements of the clause's structure. The differences between this kind of 'subject' and the more usual kind of subject outweigh the similarities and it is better not to think of the imperative kind of 'subject' as a subject at all.

The choice of the term major in preference to the term minor is realised by the presence of a predicator in the structure of a clause. The choice of the term minor in preference to the term major is realised by the absence of a predicator from the structure of a clause.

The three clauses of

Ex. 8^1.30 A   *Would you like black coffee?*
           B   *I should prefer white, if you don't mind*

have each chosen major. Each clause has a predicator.
The three clauses of

Ex. 8^1.29 A   *Black coffee?*
           B   *White, please*

have each chosen minor. None of the clauses has a predicator.

Some terms are realised not by the presence or absence of a particular element of structure but by the position of particular elements in the sequence of elements of a structure.

For instance, the term declarative is realised by the structure SP in

contrast with the term interrogative which is realised by the structure PS
or P(S); that is, the term declarative is realised by the occurrence of the
subject of a clause in front of the predicator, while the term interrogative
is realised by the occurrence of some or all of the predicator in front of
the subject.

The clauses

Ex. 8^1.92   *The post has come*
Ex. 2.2   *I want some string*
Ex. 8^1.94   *John is in London*

have chosen declarative. In each the subject comes before the predicator.
The clauses

Ex. 8^1.95   *Has the post come?*
Ex. 8^1.96   *Have you any string?*
Ex. 8^1.97   *Where is John?*

have chosen interrogative. Ex. 8^1.95 has the structure P(S). Ex. 8^1.96 and
97 each have the structure PS.

The realisations of the terms declarative and interrogative are really
more complex than the above paragraphs make them appear since
intonation and the presence or absence of a *wh-* word also need to be
taken into account.

Another example of a system whose terms are realised by the position
of particular elements in the sequence of elements of a structure is the
system unmarked theme/marked theme. The term unmarked theme is realised by the occurrence of the element subject at the beginning of a clause.
The term marked theme is realised by the occurrence of the complement,
adjunct or part of the predicator in front of the subject.

The clauses

Ex. 8^1.66   *I shall complete this tomorrow or Friday*
Ex. 8^1.67   *You can find shells on the sea-shore*
Ex. 8^1.68   *(And) they ran all the way home*

have chosen unmarked theme. Each has its subject at the beginning.
The clauses

Ex. 8^1.69   *This I shall complete tomorrow or Friday*
Ex. 8^1.70   *On the sea-shore you can find shells*
Ex. 8^1.71   *(And) run they did all the way home*

have chosen marked theme. Ex. 8^1.69 has its complement in front of its subject. Ex. 8^1.70 has an adjunct in front of its subject. Ex. 8^1.71 has part of its predicator in front of its subject.

It should be noted that the part of the predicator which occurs in front of the subject in the realisation of marked theme is a different part of the predicator from that which occurs in front of the subject in the realisation of the term interrogative.

In addition to the presence or absence of a particular element and the sequence of particular elements, there are other ways in which structures can realise terms from systems. These other ways will be discussed later in the chapter. At the moment the main point which is being made is simply that there is a realisation relationship between system and structure.

2.2.2   *Realisation Relationships between the Structures and Formal Items of Grammar*

The relationship between the structures and formal items of grammar is that elements of structure are realised by formal items, or, to put it the other way, that formal items realise elements of structure.

This was implied in Chapter 5 of Volume 1 when it was said that formal items represent elements of structure. It was also indicated in Chapter 5 of Volume 1 that structures and formal items were of different orders of abstraction. What was really meant by this was that structures and formal items were at different points on the scale of realisation.

Since formal items realise elements of structure and since structures realise terms from systems, formal items can be said to realise terms from systems indirectly via structures.

Sometimes when formal items realise structures which realise terms from systems, the structures are more important in the realisation process than the formal items. Sometimes the formal items are more important than the structures.

The clause

Ex. 2.3   *Are you coming?*

has chosen the term interrogative from the system declarative/interrogative. The term interrogative is realised by the P(S) order of the elements of structure of the clause. The elements S and P are realised by the formal items *you* and *are coming*.

Here the structure is more important in the realisation process than the formal items, since it is the order of elements of structure which really gives the clue to the fact that the term interrogative has been chosen. Of course it is true that the formal items are important in that the elements of structure must be realised by something. But it does not matter which formal items are doing the realising. Any nominal group can realise S and any verbal group can realise P.

It is true for all the terms whose realisations were discussed in Section 2.2.1 that structure plays a more important part in the realisation process than the formal items.

However, the clause

Ex. 8^1.10   *Theodore saw Mary on Tuesday*

has chosen the term mental process. The term mental process is realised by the fact that the clause's predicator is realised by the formal item *saw,* a formal item belonging to a particular sub-class of the verbal group.

Here the formal item is more important in the realisation process than the structure. The structure is important in that the clause must have a predicator in order for the distinction between material process, mental process and relational process to be made explicitly. But what really makes the distinction is that a formal item from a particular sub-class of formal items has been chosen to realise the predicator.

The clause Ex. 8^1.10 has also chosen the term internalised process and the term perception process. The term internalised process is realised by the fact that the predicator is realised by a formal item chosen from a particular sub-class of the sub-class used to realise the term mental process. The term perception process is realised by the fact that the predicator is realised by a formal item chosen from a particular sub-class of the sub-class used to realise the term internalised process (a sub-class of a sub-class of the sub-class used to realise the term mental process).

The realisation relationships within the level of grammar, as discussed so far, are shown in Figure 2.3.

FIGURE 2.3   *The realisation relationships within the level of grammar (a)*

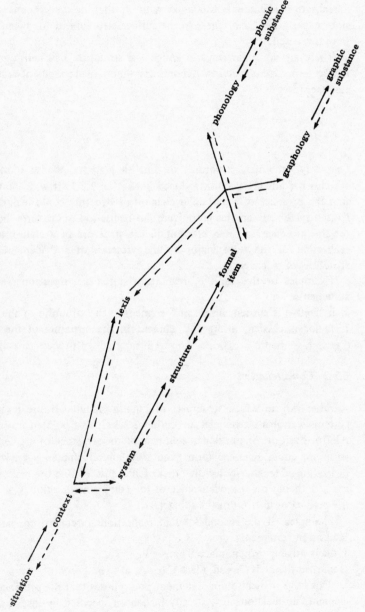

2.3   REALISATION STATEMENTS

In a systemic grammar of a language each term from a system should have a **realisation statement** associated with it; that is, the grammar should state exactly how and where in the surface structure of the language the term is realised.

There are six main ways in which the structures of English grammar realise terms from systems. Accordingly there are six kinds of realisation statement.

2.3.1 *Insertion*

One way in which structures of English grammar realise terms from systems has already been introduced in Section 2.2.1. It was pointed out that the presence of a particular element of structure could realise a term from a system. Examples given were the realisation of the term indicative by the presence of an S element in the structure of a clause, and the realisation of the term major by the presence of a P element in the structure of a clause.

Examples of this kind of realisation statement, **insertion** realisation statements, are:

If indicative is chosen, insert an S element in the structure of the clause.
If major is chosen, insert a P element in the structure of the clause.

2.3.2 *Concatenation*

Another way in which structures of English grammar realise terms from systems was also introduced in Section 2.2.1. It was pointed out that the relative position of particular elements in the sequence of elements of a structure could realise a term from a system. Examples given were the realisation of declarative by the order of elements SP, and the realisation of marked theme by the occurrence of the complement, adjunct or part of the predicator in front of the subject.

Examples of the second kind of realisation statement, **concatenation** realisation statements, are:

If declarative is chosen, place S before P.
If marked theme is chosen, place C (or A, or v) before S.

This kind of realisation statement presupposes that the presence of the elements in question must already have been specified by insertion realisation statements relating to terms from less delicate systems.

2.3.3 *Particularisation*

A third way in which structures of English grammar realise terms from systems was introduced in Section 2.2.2. It was pointed out that a term from a system could be realised by the selection of a formal item from a particular sub-class of formal items. Examples given of terms realised in this way were the terms mental process, internalised process and perception process.

Examples of the third kind of realisation statement, **particularisation** realisation statements, are:

If the term mental process is chosen, represent the element P by a formal item from the mental sub-class of verbal groups.

If the term internalised process is chosen, represent the element P by a formal item from the internal sub-class (of the mental sub-class) of verbal groups.

If the term perception process is chosen, represent the element P by a formal item from the perception sub-class (of the internal sub-class of the mental sub-class) of verbal groups.

This kind of realisation statement, like the second kind, presupposes that the presence of the element in question must already have been specified by an insertion realisation statement relating to a term from a less delicate system.

2.3.4 *Inclusion*

The fourth, fifth and sixth ways in which structures of English grammar realise terms from systems have not yet been discussed in this chapter, although examples were given of them in Volume 1.

Before we can consider these last three ways, we need to make a further modification to our realisation scale. The version of the scale given in Figure 2.3 is incomplete.

In Chapter 5 of Volume 1 (Section 2.5) the notion of functions was introduced. We have not yet seen how functions fit onto the scale of realisation.

Functions in fact come between systems and structures on the scale (see Figure 2.4).

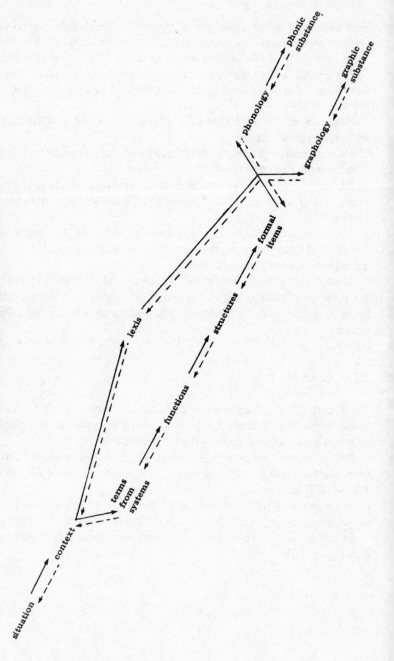

FIGURE 2.4   *The realisation relationships within the level of grammar (b)*

Let us take as examples of functions some of the participant roles mentioned in Sections 8.4.1 and 8.4.2 of Volume 1.

Certain choices from the transitivity systems specify the inclusion in the message of certain participant roles. For instance if a material process clause has chosen the term middle, the message includes a participant in the role of actor. If a material process clause has chosen the term non-middle, the message includes both a participant in the role of actor and a participant in the role of goal.

Examples of the fourth kind of realisation statement, **inclusion** realisation statements, are:

If the term middle is chosen, include the function actor.

If the term non-middle is chosen, include the function actor and the function goal.

As may be expected from the fact that functions are nearer to systems on the realisation scale than are structures or formal items, inclusion realisation statements are logically prior to the kinds of realisation statement previously discussed. The kinds of realisation statement previously discussed presuppose inclusion realisation statements. For instance the insertion realisation statements 'If indicative is chosen insert an S element in the structure of the clause' and 'If major is chosen insert a P element in the structure of the clause' presuppose respectively the inclusion realisation statements 'Include the function mood marker[1]' and 'Include the function process'.

2.3.5 *Conflation*

As was stated in the previous section, non-middle material process clauses include both a participant in the role of actor and a participant in the role of goal. This does not mean however that a non-middle material process clause must explicitly include both these functions. It may include one of them implicitly.

As we saw in Section 8.4.2 of Volume 1 both the non-middle clauses

Ex. 8[1].51   *Cover point threw wildly to the wicket keeper*
Ex. 8[1].57   *The ball was thrown to the wicket keeper*

include both actor and goal, although Ex. 8[1].51 makes only its actor explicit leaving its goal implicit, while Ex. 8[1].57 makes only its goal explicit leaving its actor implicit. These clauses have included exactly the same functions as

Ex. 8^1.48   *Cover point threw the ball wildly to the wicket keeper*
Ex. 8^1.54   *The ball was thrown to the wicket keeper by cover point*

All four clauses have followed the inclusion realisation statement:
If the term non-middle is chosen, include the function actor and the function goal.

The difference between the former pair and the latter pair lies in whether or not the inclusion realisation statement is followed by an insertion realisation statement. Ex. 8^1.48 makes its goal explicit. For this clause the inclusion realisation statement is followed by the insertion realisation statement: Realise goal by inserting a C element into the structure of the clause. This insertion realisation statement does not apply to Ex. 8^1.51 since Ex. 8^1.51 leaves its goal implicit. Ex. 8^1.54 makes its actor explicit. For this clause the inclusion realisation statement is followed by the insertion realisation statement: Realise actor by inserting an A element into the structure of the clause. This insertion realisation statement does not apply to Ex. 8^1.57 since Ex. 8^1.57 leaves its actor implicit.

The kind of choice we noted in Section 8.4.2 of Volume 1 between making a function explicit and leaving it implicit is realised, then, by following an inclusion realisation statement with an insertion realisation statement if explicit is chosen, and by not following an inclusion realisation statement with an insertion realisation statement if implicit is chosen.

We also noted in Section 8.4.2 of Volume 1 another kind of choice. We noted that, given that a particular function is to be made explicit, there is sometimes a choice as to where in the clause to represent the function. The example given of this kind of choice was the active/passive system.

So far in the present section we have been contrasting Ex. 8^1.51 and Ex. 8^1.57 with Ex. 8^1.48 and Ex. 8^1.54. Let us now pair these examples rather differently and apply a different kind of contrast. Let us pair Ex. 8^1.51 with 8^1.48 and contrast this pair with Ex. 8^1.57 and 8^1.54. The difference between the two pairs is of course that Ex. 8^1.51 and Ex. 8^1.48 have chosen the term active while Ex. 8^1.57 and Ex. 8^1.54 have chosen the term passive.

How are these terms realised?

This brings us to our fifth kind of realisation statement.

The S element of a clause always realises the function mood marker[1]. (See Volume 1, Sections 5.2.5 and 5.2.6.) In the four clauses with which we are at present concerned the S elements are all realising the function mood marker[1].

In Ex. 8^1.51 and Ex. 8^1.48, as well as realising the function mood marker[1], the S elements are also realising the function actor. The function actor has been conflated with the function mood marker[1].

In Ex. $8^1$57. and Ex. 8^1.54, as well as realising the function mood marker[1], the S elements are also realising the function goal. The function goal has been conflated with the function mood marker[1].

An active clause, then, conflates its actor with the function mood marker[1]. If it realises its goal at all it does so, as we saw earlier in the section, by inserting a separate C element into the clause. A passive clause on the other hand conflates its goal with the function mood marker[1]. If it realises its actor at all it does so, again as we saw earlier in the section, by inserting a separate A element into the clause.

Examples of the fifth kind of realisation statement, **conflation** realisation statements, are:

If the term active is chosen, conflate the function actor with the function mood marker[1].

If the term passive is chosen, conflate the function goal with the function mood marker[1].

Conflation realisation statements presuppose inclusion realisation statements.

2.3.6 *Discontinuity*

We have seen that a given element of structure can realise more than one function. The reverse is also true. A given function can be realised by more than one element of structure.

The choice of the term episodes parallel (see Section 8.4.6 of Volume 1) specifies the inclusion of the function **co-ordinator.** This is realised by the insertion of a particular class of adjunct, as for example *or* in

Ex. 8^1.132   *Speak now or forever hold your peace*
Ex. 8^1.148   *He fell or was pushed*

As we saw in Section 8.4.6 of Volume 1, complex clauses which have chosen episodes parallel go on to make a further choice between non-emphatic and emphatic. The complex clauses

Ex. 8^1.149   *Either speak now or forever hold your peace*
Ex. 8^1.133   *He either fell or was pushed*

have chosen emphatic. The term emphatic is realised by splitting the function co-ordinator into two halves and by inserting two adjuncts each realising one half of the function.

Similarly clauses which have chosen modality assessed and almost certain (see Section 8.4.5 of Volume 1) have a non-emphatic/emphatic option open to them. The clauses

Ex. 8^1.110　　*It must be raining*
Ex. 2.4　　　　*He must be here by now*

have chosen non-emphatic. The clauses

Ex. 2.5　　　　*It must certainly be raining*
Ex. 8^1.118　　*He must certainly be here by now*

have chosen emphatic.

The term modality assessed specifies the inclusion of the function **degree of certainty**. In the non-emphatic examples this function is conflated with the function process and realised in the predicator. In the emphatic examples the function degree of certainty is split into two, and one half of it is conflated with the process while the other half of it is realised by the insertion of an adjunct into the structure of the clause.

Examples of the sixth kind of realisation statement, **discontinuity** realisation statements, are:

If the choice of the term episodes parallel is followed by the choice of the term emphatic, split the function co-ordinator into co-ordinator^1 and co-ordinator^2.

If the choice of the term almost certain is followed by the choice of the term emphatic, split the function degree of certainty into degree of certainty^1 and degree of certainty^2.

Discontinuity realisation statements, like conflation, insertion, concatenation and particularisation realisation statements, presuppose inclusion realisation statements.

It may perhaps be helpful at this point to summarise what has been said about the realisation of terms from systems within the level of grammar and to make explicit some things which have so far only been implied:

Each choice which is made from a system acts as the signal for a move on the scale of realisation. Any utterance involves a series of such choices and a series of such moves, each move taking the utterance a step nearer to the audible or visible manifestation of its message.

At the level of grammar the moves in the process of realisation can be divided into stages since they occur in a certain relative order. The stages are as follows:

1. The inclusion of certain specified functions.
2. The splitting up of any of these functions which are to be discontinuous.
3. The conflation of any functions (or parts of functions) which are to be conflated.
4. The realisation of the functions (or in the case of conflated functions the realisation of the bundles of functions) by the insertion of elements of structure.
5. The concatenation of the elements of structure.
6. The realisation of the elements of structure by formal items chosen from particular classes or sub-classes.

By means of moves at these various stages the structure of an utterance is built up so that the utterance has form as well as meaning. Eventually, by a continuation of the process of realisation through the level of phonology or graphology, the utterance also acquires substance.

Movement along the realisation scale is, then, movement from the meanings of language, the fundamental things of language, to the form and substance, the surface things of language, showing by what stages the one is encoded in the other.

2.4 REALISATION, RANK AND DELICACY

2.4.1 *Realisation and Rank*

It was indicated in Chapter 7 of Volume 1 that unit was related to system in two ways. The first of these ways was introduced in Chapters 8 and 9 of Volume 1 when it was shown that units provided entry conditions for systems, points of origin for networks.

The second way in which unit is related to system is that units provide the domains within which terms from systems are realised. Each system has a particular rank of unit as entry condition, and each term is realised at a particular rank (or ranks) of unit.

Most of the systems used as examples in Section 2.3 of the present chapter have the clause as entry condition and are also realised at the rank of clause. For instance the declarative/interrogative system, as indicated in Chapters 8 and 9 of Volume 1, has the clause as entry condition. It is also realised at the rank of clause, by the order of elements of clause structure.

It is not always the case however that the rank of unit which acts as entry condition for a system also provides the domain within which the system's terms are realised. It is quite possible for a term from a system to be chosen at one rank (i.e. to have one rank as the system's entry condition) and to be realised at another rank. For instance the term almost certain is chosen, as indicated in Chapters 8 and 9 of Volume 1, at the rank of clause. As indicated in Section 2.3.6 of the present chapter this term is partially realised at the rank of clause in the inclusion of the function degree of certainty, the conflation of this function with the function process, and the realisation of the resulting bundle of functions by the insertion of a predicator into the structure of the clause. However the further realisation of the term almost certain is at a lower rank, by means of the insertion of the element auxiliary verb into the structure of a group and by the particularisation of this element of structure, a formal item from a particular sub-class of word being chosen to represent it.

It is important to stress that although this book has tended to concentrate on the clause when giving examples, partly because the clause is the unit which has so far been studied in greatest detail, nevertheless it is equally true that each of the other ranks of unit similarly provides points of origin and domains of realisation.

Rank is sometimes confused with realisation, perhaps because many terms from systems are realised or partially realised at a rank lower than the rank at which they are chosen so that the impression is sometimes gained that one always moves down the scale of rank at the same time as one moves along the scale of realisation.

Certainly there is a general tendency for downward movement on the rank scale to accompany movement along the realisation scale. But there is no one-to-one correspondence between a step on the rank scale and a step on the scale of realisation. Different terms move down a rank at different stages in their realisation processes. The path of a given term along the realisation scale can only be adequately mapped if the scales of rank and realisation are treated as distinct.

The following diagrams show the paths along the realisation scale of some of the terms from systems used as examples in this chapter. Each diagram shows in bold type the crucial stage of realisation for a given term; that is, it shows the move in the realisation process for which the given term acts as the signal. As well as the crucial stage of realisation for the given term, each diagram also shows the moves specified by other terms which are presupposed by the given term. Where relevant the moves specified by other terms which are assumed to follow the crucial stage are also shown. (As usual it has been necessary to oversimplify for the sake of clarity.)

FIGURE 2.5 *The path of the term mental process along the scale of realisation and down the scale of rank*

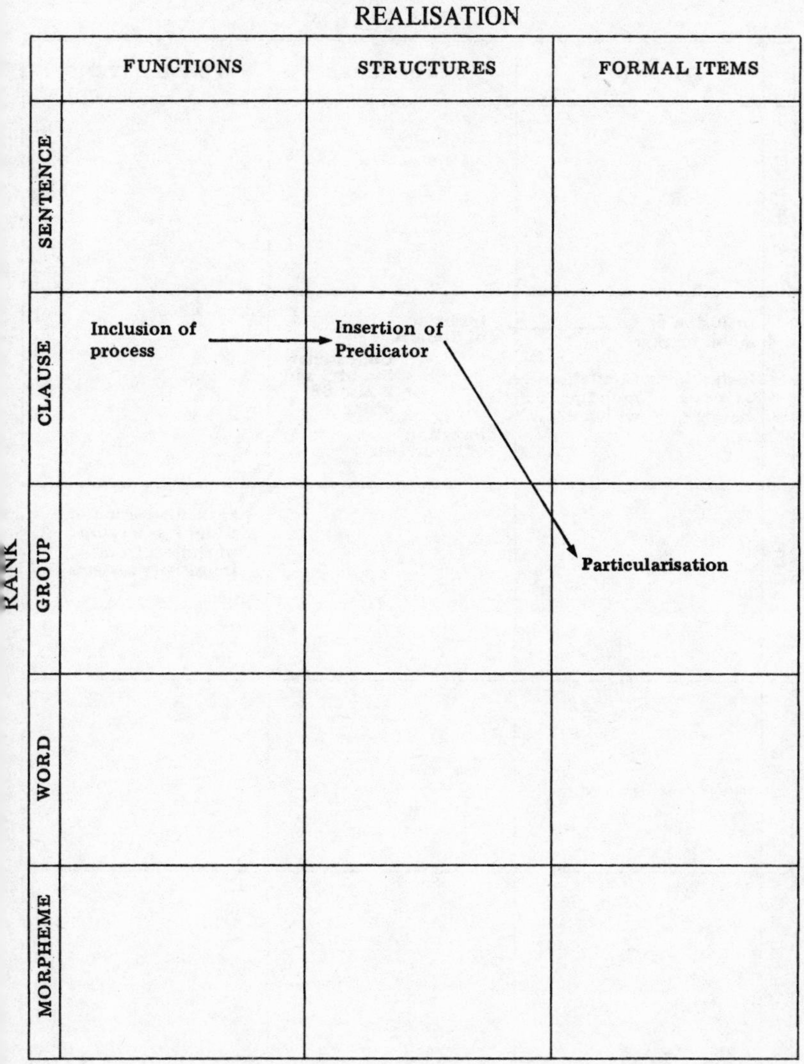

REALISATION

	FUNCTIONS	STRUCTURES	FORMAL ITEMS
SENTENCE			
CLAUSE	Inclusion of process	Insertion of Predicator	
GROUP			Particularisation
WORD			
MORPHEME			

RANK

FIGURE 2.6 *The path of the term declarative along the scale of realisation and down the scale of rank*

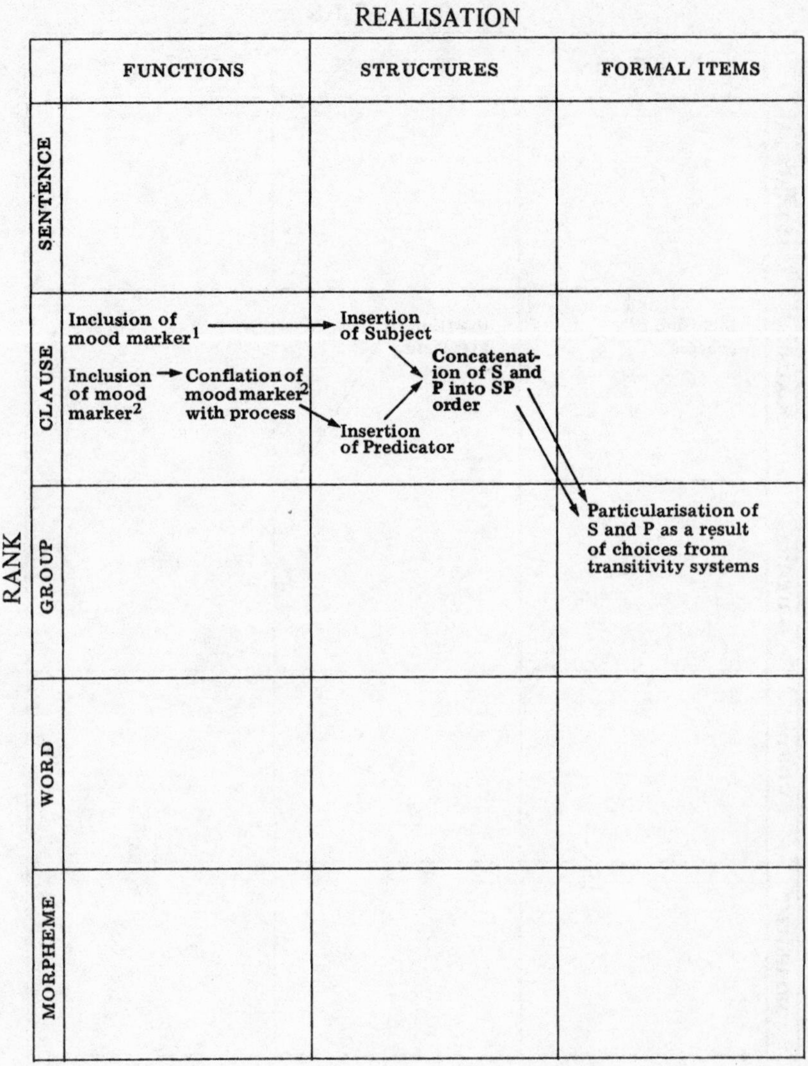

REALISATION

		FUNCTIONS	STRUCTURES	FORMAL ITEMS
RANK	**SENTENCE**			
	CLAUSE	Inclusion of mood marker[1] → Inclusion → Conflation of of mood mood marker[2] marker[2] with process	→ Insertion of Subject Concatenation of S and P into SP order → Insertion of Predicator	
	GROUP			↘ Particularisation of S and P as a result of choices from transitivity systems
	WORD			
	MORPHEME			

FIGURE 2.7 *The path of the term almost certain along the scale of realisation and down the scale of rank*

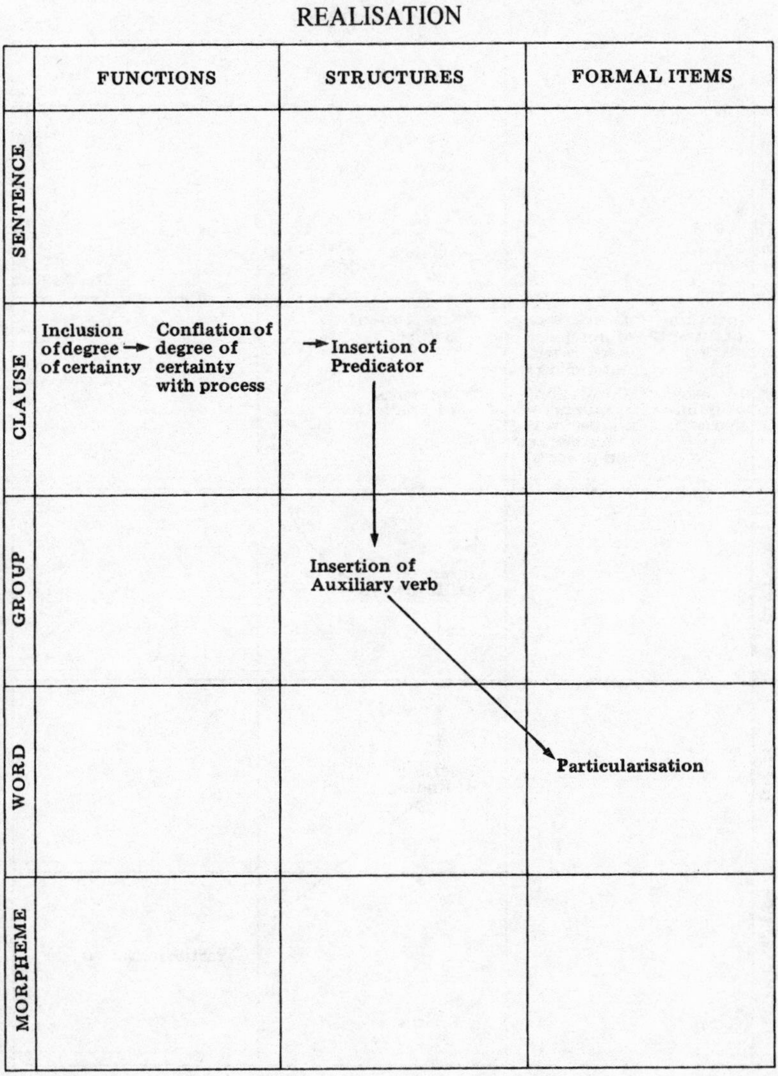

REALISATION

	FUNCTIONS	STRUCTURES	FORMAL ITEMS
SENTENCE			
CLAUSE	Inclusion of degree of certainty → Conflation of degree of certainty with process	→ Insertion of Predicator	
GROUP		Insertion of Auxiliary verb	
WORD			Particularisation
MORPHEME			

FIGURE 2.8 *The path of the term plural along the scale of realisation and down the scale of rank*

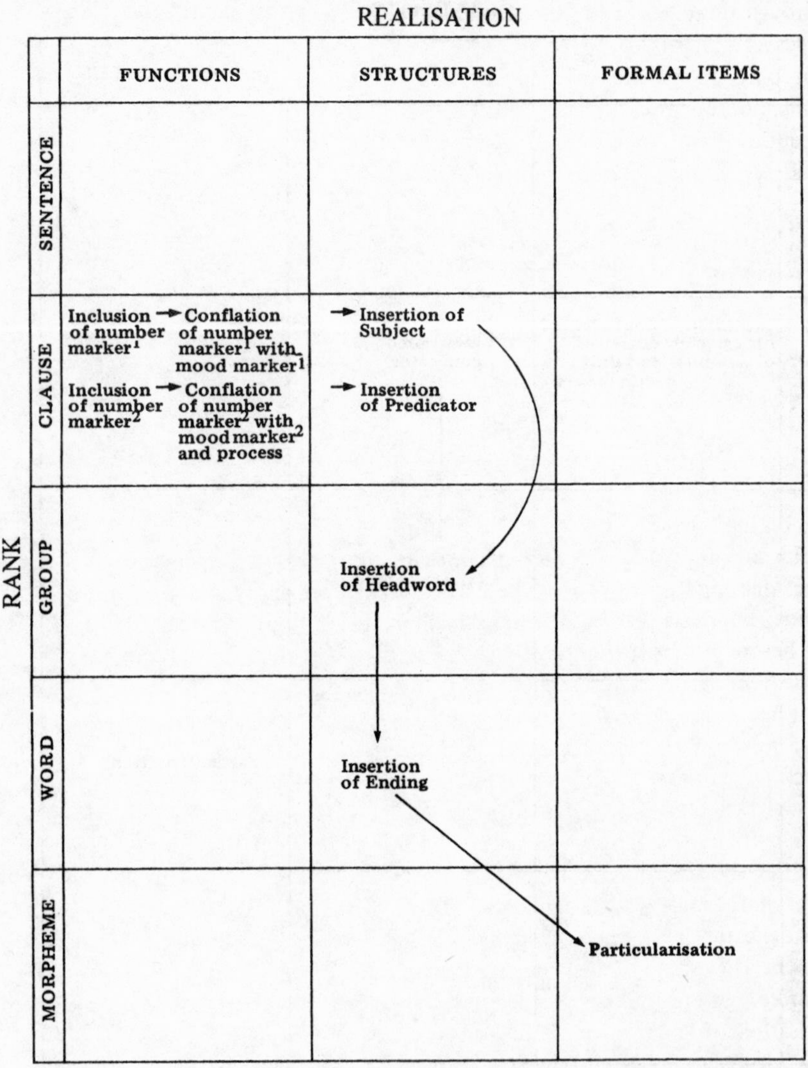

REALISATION

	FUNCTIONS	STRUCTURES	FORMAL ITEMS
SENTENCE			
CLAUSE	Inclusion → Conflation of number of number marker¹ marker¹ with mood marker¹ Inclusion → Conflation of number of number marker² marker² with, mood marker² and process	→ Insertion of Subject → Insertion of Predicator	
GROUP		Insertion of Headword	
WORD		Insertion of Ending	
MORPHEME			Particularisation

RANK

Note: This diagram relates to the number system whose entry condition is the clause. There are other number systems with other entry conditions.

The scales of rank and realisation are distinct, then, in that movement on one scale does not necessarily coincide with movement on the other.

That the two scales are distinct is further indicated by the fact that, although there has been no room to demonstrate this in this book, all the stages of realisation can be discussed in relation to all the ranks of unit. Not only do clauses have functions, elements of structure and formal items; so too do sentences, groups and words. (The morpheme is the exception here. As discussed in Chapter 6 of Volume 1, since it is the smallest grammatical unit, it does not have elements of structure.)

2.4.2 Realisation and Delicacy

Similarly realisation and delicacy are sometimes confused. This confusion perhaps arises because there is a tendency for more delicate systems to specify moves nearer the surface end of the realisation scale, so that again an impression is gained of movement on the two scales simultaneously.

However again it must be stressed that the two scales are distinct. Again there is no one-to-one correspondence between a step on one scale and a step on the other.

For the purpose of considering the process of realisation we assume that all of one kind of move must be carried out before another kind of move begins. For instance we assume that all inclusion moves must be carried out before any insertion moves begin, and that all insertion moves must be carried out before any particularisation moves begin.

If we consider terms from the point of view of their delicacy, we find ourselves considering them in a different order from the order in which we consider them if we are primarily concerned with the realisation moves which they specify. It is true that a term which specifies the inclusion of a particular function will always be less delicate than a term which specifies the insertion of the element realising that function, and that a term which specifies the insertion of a particular element will always be less delicate than a term which specifies the particularisation of that element. However a term specifying the inclusion of one function may well be more delicate than terms specifying the inclusion, insertion and partic-ularisation of another function. For instance in the transitivity and voice network given in Chapter 9 of Volume 1, the term non-middle, which specifies the inclusion of the functions actor and goal, is more delicate than terms specifying the inclusion, insertion and particularisation of the function process.

The scales of realisation and delicacy, then, result in different orderings of terms from systems.

It should also be stressed that, although different terms specify moves at different stages of the realisation process, all the terms themselves, no matter what the delicacy of their systems, are at the same point on the realisation scale. All terms from systems are semantic.* They are all at the extreme end of the grammatical section of the realisation scale, before meanings have begun to be converted into forms.

In the systemic model of language, then, delicacy, rank and realisation are three distinct but intersecting scales, designed to account for different kinds of relationship in language. Delicacy is designed primarily to account for semantic relationships, relationships between meanings (see Chapter 9 of Volume 1). Rank is designed primarily, though not entirely, to account for status relationships, relationships between forms (see Chapter 7 of Volume 1). Realisation is designed to show the stages by which the forms of language are derived from the meanings of language.

2.5   REALISATION AND THE AXES OF CHAIN AND CHOICE

So far in this book we have tended to consider the axis of chain mainly in relation to formal items and structures, the most surface things on the grammatical section of the scale of realisation, while we have tended to consider the axis of choice mainly in relation to meanings, the most fundamental things on the grammatical section of the scale. Chapters 5, 6 and 7 of Volume 1 focussed on the link between the axis of chain and formal items and structures. Chapters 8 and 9 of Volume 1 focussed on the link between the axis of choice and the meanings, the terms from systems.

Let us now consider how far this linking of chain with the most surface things and of choice with the most fundamental things is justified.

2.5.1   *Realisation and the Axis of Choice*

Let us first consider the linking of the axis of choice with the most fundamental things.

Certainly we saw in Chapters 8 and 9 of Volume 1 that we do make choices between different meanings. However we not only make choices between meanings. We also make choices at the more surface points on the realisation scale; we make choices between functions, choices between structures, choices between classes of formal items.

*More accurately, all terms from the systems discussed in this book are semantic. There are other kinds of system.

Why has this book not devoted as much attention to the more surface kinds of choice as it has to the choices between meanings? Partly from lack of space, partly just because meanings are the most fundamental, the most important, things of language, but perhaps mostly because the more surface choices are determined by the meaning choices and therefore there is a sense in which there is no need to discuss the more surface choices if we have fully explored the meaning choices.*

It is as if we were about to go for a walk and made all the decisions about our route before setting out. Once actually on the walk no further decisions would be necessary as all the turnings we were to take would have been pre-selected. On the walk itself we should simply have to implement our earlier decisions.

When we choose terms from systems we are not only making choices between different meanings; we are also making choices between different paths along the realisation scale consequent upon the choices between different meanings. All the decisions are made at the most fundamental point on the realisation scale. As we move nearer the surface on the scale we may appear to be making further decisions but in reality we are simply implementing earlier decisions. All the choices we make between functions, structures and classes of formal items are the direct result of the choices we made between terms from systems.

The axis of choice is, then, relevant to the whole of the scale of realisation, not just to the terms-from-systems point on the scale, as may have appeared from the previous chapters of the book. But its relevance does not lie in choices being made equally at all points on the scale. Its relevance lies in the fact that a particular path along the whole scale is chosen in preference to another path along the whole scale as a result of choices between different meanings.

2.5.2 Realisation and the Axis of Chain

Let us now consider the linking of the axis of chain with the most surface things.

At the beginning of Chapter 4 of Volume 1 the axis of chain was introduced as the axis which accounts for the relationships between things occurring one after another sequentially in time or space. Certainly if this is our definition of the axis of chain then it can be applied to formal items

*By no means all systemicists would agree with the point of view expressed here. Some systemicists are much more interested in exploring the systems of contrasting choices at other levels of language than they are in the meaning choices which have been discussed in this book.

and structures since, as shown in Chapter 5 of Volume 1, formal items and elements of structure do occur one after another in time or space.

It is less easy to apply it to functions since, although some functions occur sequentially, others, as we have seen, are conflated into bundles of functions. Some of the links in our chain are now occurring on top of each other rather than in line.

It is even less easy to apply this view of the axis of chain to terms from systems.

However if we changed the emphasis of our definition of the axis of chain slightly, as we did towards the end of Chapter 4 of Volume 1, we should be able to apply it to the more fundamental things of grammar as well as to the more surface things.

We should need to drop our insistence on the 'things occurring one after another sequentially in time or space' and say instead simply that the axis of chain accounts for the relationships between things actually present in a given utterance (as opposed to the axis of choice which accounts for the relationships between the things which are present and the things which might have been present but which are absent).

We could still apply this new view of the axis of chain to formal items and structures. The formal items of a given utterance are things actually present in the utterance. So too are the elements of structure.

We can now apply the concept to functions since the functions of a given utterance are things actually present in the utterance, even if they do not occur sequentially.

We can also apply the concept to terms from systems. The terms actually chosen by a given utterance, the meanings, can be regarded as things present in the utterance.

(Sometimes a terminological distinction is made between terms viewed from the axis of choice and terms viewed from the axis of chain. The word *term* is reserved for a term viewed as being in contrast with other terms on the axis of choice. A term which has actually been chosen by a given utterance, and which is present in the utterance together with other terms to which it is related on the axis of chain, is called a **feature**. Thus for example indicative is called a *term* if it is being viewed primarily as something which contrasts with imperative. It is called a *feature* if it is being viewed primarily as something actually chosen by a given utterance together with other features such as major, material process and marked theme.)

Neither the axis of choice nor the axis of chain, then, belongs exclusively to any one point on the scale of realisation, though each is perhaps more applicable at one end of the scale than at the other.

We now have two more dimensions to add to the three whose interrelations were discussed in the previous section.

We have seen in this section that realisation is related to both chain and choice.

We have seen that realisation is related to chain in that in any utterance a 'chain' of things actually present can be said to occur at each point on the scale of realisation; in any utterance there will be a 'chain' of features, a 'chain' of functions, a chain of elements of structure, a chain of formal items. These 'chains' are related to each other by the scale of realisation, each 'chain' being realised by the 'chain' a step nearer to the surface than itself.

We have seen that realisation is related to choice in that the paths along the scale of realisation are things between which we choose. The paths along the scale of realisation chosen by a particular utterance contrast with the paths which might have been chosen but which have not been chosen. At each point on the scale the 'chain' of things present contrast with the things which might have been present but which are absent, the most important of these contrasts being those between the features of the utterance and the other terms of their respective systems.

Delicacy can similarly be regarded as relating to both chain and choice.

Delicacy both accounts for relationships within the 'chain' of features actually chosen by a given utterance and accounts for the relationships between systems, the terms of which contrast with each other on the axis of choice.

We saw in Chapter 7 of Volume 1 that rank is related to both chain and choice in that it can be regarded as accounting for relationships between formal items actually occurring in utterances, relationships on the axis of chain, or as accounting for relationships between formal items in their potential for occurring in utterances, relationships on the axis of choice.

To put into perspective the main points made in this section and the previous section:

Any given utterance chooses a path (or paths) along the scale of delicacy; that is, it chooses a 'chain' of features which are related on the scale of delicacy. This path along the scale of delicacy contrasts on the axis of choice with the paths on the scale which might have been chosen but which have not been chosen.

As a result of its choice of a path along the scale of delicacy, the utterance also chooses a path (or paths) along the scale of realisation; that is, as a result of its choice of a 'chain' of features, it also chooses a 'chain' of functions, a chain of elements of structure and a chain of formal items, these 'chains' being related on the scale of realisation. The path along the scale of realisation, like the path along the scale of delicacy, contrasts on

FIGURE 2.9 *The five main dimensions of the systemic model of grammar*

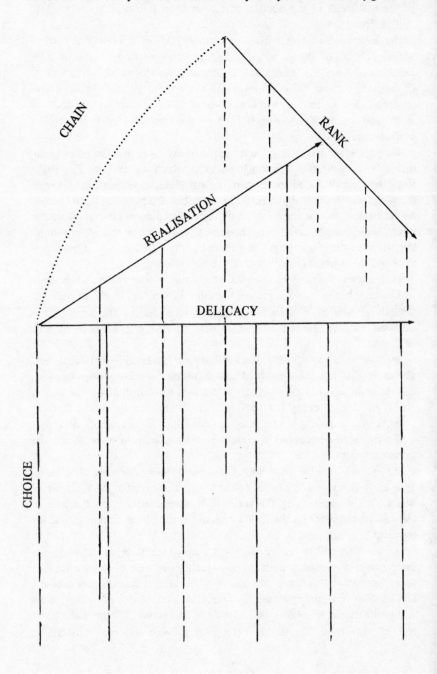

the axis of choice with the paths on the scale which might have been chosen but which have not been chosen.

The formal items actually occurring in the chain at the far end of the grammatical section of the utterance's path along the scale of realisation are of different size and status; they are relatable on the scale of rank. The ranks of unit actually chosen by the utterance contrast on the axis of choice with other ranks of unit and with other members of the same unit. (Sometimes it is the contrast between different ranks of unit which is important, as suggested in the extract at the beginning of Section 8.4.6 of Volume 1. More often it is the contrast between different classes and sub-classes of the same unit.)

Multidimensional diagrams are difficult to draw. Figure 2.9 attempts to show the different dimensions of systemic grammar. The dashed lines leading from the scales are intended to show that each scale relates to the axis of choice as well as to the axis of chain. The dotted loop-back from rank is intended as a reminder that units not only act as the realisations of terms but also provide points of origin for networks.

It should be emphasised that the scale of realisation, like the scale of delicacy, has no chronological implication. The scale has been introduced in this chapter as a series of stages taking a speaker or writer from the things he wants to express to the means of expressing them. These stages are however theoretical stages designed to account for the relationships between different aspects of language. They do not necessarily imply that a speaker or writer (or hearer or reader) either consciously or subconsciously moves along the scale from one stage to the next in chronological order.

If we were to try to relate the scale of realisation to the psychological processes of the human mind we should probably want to hypothesise that shunting takes place along the realisation scale, as indeed along the scales of rank and delicacy. Certainly we have to assume theoretical shunting on the scale of realisation since, as we have seen, units not only result from choices from systems but also condition them.

2.6   DISCUSSION

2.6.1   *General Linguistics*

In Chapters 5, 6 and 7 of Volume 1 we were mainly concerned with the surface things of language, the forms. In Chapters 8 and 9 of Volume 1 we were mainly concerned with the more fundamental things of language,

tne meanings. In this chapter we have been concerned with the relationships between forms and meanings.

We have been looking at the ways in which the forms of utterances are
derived from the meanings. We have seen that each meaning choice specifies
a move on the scale of realisation leading to the form of the utterance. We
have seen that in this way the meanings are encoded in the forms.

We can say that at the level of grammar language consists of meaning
and form, the form being determined by the meaning. We can say that
language works by encoding its meaning in its form through a series of
stages. In all languages form is determined by meaning and in all languages
form encodes meaning.

2.6.2 *Descriptive Linguistics*

As indicated in Chapter 9 of Volume 1, when we are describing the
grammar of a language (or a variety of a language) the most important
thing we have to do is to codify the meaning potential of the grammar of
that language; we have to show what meanings it is possible for the grammar
of the language to express and how these meanings relate to each other.

Codifying the meaning potential is the most important task in the description of a language, but it is not the only task. We also have to show
how the meanings relate to the forms; we have to show, that is, how the
things that the speakers of the language 'can mean' relate to the things that
they 'can say', how meaning potential relates to saying potential. We have
to show by what stages along the realisation scale each of the things that the
speakers of the language 'can mean' is converted into something that they
'can say'.

Meaning potential and saying potential, together with certain aspects
of extra-linguistic behaviour, add up to the behaviour potential
mentioned in Section 2.1.2 of Volume 1. For further discussion of
this see Halliday 1971 and Turner 1972.

When we are describing a whole language (or a whole variety of language)
we are concerned with potential meaning, potential saying and the potential
realisation relationships between them; it is the axis of choice which is all
important.

When we are describing particular utterances both the axis of chain and
the axis of choice are important. The axis of chain is our primary concern;
we are concerned with actual meanings, actual forms and the actual
realisation relationships between them. The axis of choice is also relevant
however in that potential sheds light on actual. The meanings, forms

and realisation relationships actually present in an utterance contrast with those which might have been present but are absent. When we describe particular utterances we consider the 'means' and the 'says' and the actual realisation relationship in the light of the 'can mean' and the 'can say' and the potential realisation relationships.

2.6.3 *Contrastive Linguistics*

Languages and varieties of languages, as indicated in Chapter 9 of Volume 1, can differ in three main ways: they can differ in their meaning potential; they can differ in the relative frequency with which their potential meanings are chosen; they can differ in the ways in which their potential meanings are realised in form.

The three ways are given here in order of likelihood. Languages and varieties of languages, at the level of grammar, are least likely to differ in meaning potential, most likely to differ in formal realisations, with relative frequency of choice somewhere in between. (Actually the likelihood varies slightly according to whether we are contrasting different languages, different dialects, different registers or different idiolects. When we are contrasting different languages the likelihood varies according to the closeness of relationship of the languages.)

The fact that meanings are the things least likely to differ while forms are the things most likely to differ means that the concept of realisation in contrastive studies often provides a useful link between the similar and the dissimilar.

In historical studies of language, for instance, one of the main aims is to show what has changed. Another of the main aims is to show what has remained the same. We frequently find in historical studies of grammar that what have remained the same are the meanings while what have changed are the forms. The concept of realisation enables us to relate the former to the latter.

2.6.4 *Applied Linguistics*

The multi-dimensional characteristic of the systemic model of language means that the overall framework of this kind of grammar sometimes seems more complicated, sometimes seems looser, than that of some other schools. However it also means that this kind of grammar is more flexible than some other kinds so that when it comes to applied linguistics, systemic grammar can be more easily adapted to a number of different purposes. For different purposes one tends to concentrate on different dimensions. For instance those systemic linguists primarily concerned with the sociological applications tend to focus their attention on the axis of choice and on the scale of delicacy, since to them the meaningful choices of language are all important. Those linguists interested in stylistics tend to pay more attention to the axis of chain and to the units and structures of language, since to them the patterns of actual utterances are particularly important. Those systemic linguists who have recently been showing some interest in the psychological aspects of language have been paying more attention than most systemic linguists to the processes of realisation, though it remains to be seen whether this dimension of systemic linguistics will be able to make a significant contribution to psychological studies.

If the present book has seemed repetitive and lacking in coherence, it is because it has aimed at providing an introduction to all the above-mentioned kinds of study rather than at giving a more unified view leading to just one kind. The book has been considering the same facts of language from a number of different standpoints, focussing in turn on each of the main dimensions of the model.

2.6.5 *Systemic Linguistics and Other Schools of Linguistics*

It was stated in Volume 1, Chapter 2 that one of the schools of linguistics with which systemic linguistics had most in common was the stratificational school. One of the concepts which these two schools share is the concept of realisation.

In fact systemic linguists owe the term *realisation* to the stratificationalists. Systemic linguists (or, as they then were, scale-and-category linguists) had earlier referred to this scale as *exponence.*

The realisation statements of systemic grammar, though formulated differently, are in their purpose not unlike the transformational rules of TG grammar. Both realisation statements and transformational rules are designed to show how the surface aspects of grammar derive from the more fundamental aspects of grammar. Systemic grammars and TG grammars do not always agree however over what counts as a surface aspect of grammar and what counts as a more fundamental aspect of grammar.

Systemic linguistics perhaps differs from other schools in the multi-dimensional and multi-purpose nature of its approach.

3
Lexis

Chapters 5-9 of Volume 1 and Chapter 2 of this volume have been concerned with the level of grammar. This chapter is concerned with the other level of linguistic form, the level of lexis.

Both grammar and lexis are concerned with formal items and with the patterns and contrasts made by formal items.

Grammar however is not concerned with the formal items per se; it is only interested in them at one remove as it were, when the formal items are realising elements of structure. Lexis on the other hand is interested in the formal items as individual formal items.

Formal items enter into the patterns of grammar, the structures, as members of classes. They enter into the patterns of lexis as individual items, not via their class properties but via their own uniqueness.

The formal contrasts of the level of grammar are made by the differences between classes of items, or by the differences between structures whose elements are realised by classes of items. The formal contrasts of the level of lexis are made by the differences between individual items or combinations of items.

3.1 COLLOCATIONS

The patterns of lexis are called **collocations.**

Collocations, like the structures of grammar, consist of 'things' occurring one after another in a sequence. For instance, just as the structure exemplified by the clause

The waitress spilt the soup on the tablecloth

consists of 'things' – the elements S, P, C, A – occurring one after another in a sequence, so too the collocation exemplified by the same utterance consists of 'things' – the items *The, waitress, spill, t, the, soup, on, the, tablecloth* – occurring one after another in a sequence. Similarly, just as the structure exemplified by the clause

I have read the first fifty pages of that book

consists of the elements S, P, C, occurring one after another in a sequence, so too the collocation exemplified by the same utterance consists of the items *I, have, read, the, first, fifty, page, s, of, that, book,* occurring one after another in a sequence.

There are, however, important differences between the collocations of lexis and the structures of grammar.

One difference between them lies in the part played by sequence in the formation of the patterns. Although, as has been shown, the 'things' which make up both kinds of pattern occur sequentially, the position of each 'thing' in the sequence is unimportant for a lexical collocation, though important for a grammatical structure. The conversation

A. *Read the first fifty pages of that book*
B. *I have*

exemplifies different grammatical structures from those of the utterance

I have read the first fifty pages of that book

but exemplifies exactly the same collocation. Similarly, a mother seeing a squabble about to arise between two of her children might say

Now, now, fair play, please John

or

Now, now, play fair John, please.

If she chose the first utterance, she would be using a different grammatical structure from the structure she would be using if she chose the second. She would be using exactly the same lexical collocation, no matter which utterance she chose.

Another difference between the collocations of lexis and the structures of grammar lies in the generality of the 'things' which make up the patterns. An element of structure is an abstraction (that is, a generalisation) from a large number of similar 'things'. For instance the element subject is a generalisation from such items as *Theodore, Tiddles, They, Alexander* and *He* in the clauses

Theodore seems fond of cats
Tiddles scratched Aunt Jemima
They like cream
Alexander plays the flute
He is musical.

These items share certain properties and therefore a general label can be applied to them all. An item of a collocation, on the other hand, is a particular unique 'thing'. For instance if, instead of considering *Theodore, Tiddles, They, Alexander* and *He* as items realising elements of structure, we consider them simply as items of collocations, we find that each is unique. Their shared properties are no longer relevant. It is the properties which make them unique which enable them to enter into collocations. Because each is unique, there is no way in which we can link them together and make a general statement about them. *Theodore* is *Theodore, Tiddles* is *Tiddles, They* is *They, Alexander* is *Alexander* and *He* is *He.* That is all we can say about them.

Just as the statements made about items of collocations are less general than the statements made about the elements of structures, so too the statements made about collocations themselves are less general than the statements made about structures. We can say of the five clauses cited in the previous paragraph that they are all alike in that they have the same structure, SPC. From a lexical point of view the five statements have nothing in common at all. If we add to these five utterances a sixth

The cat who likes music scratched Alexander

we can say that, lexically, each of the first five utterances has something in common with the sixth, in that each has a collocation which shares at least one item with the sixth. This kind of likeness between collocations is a much less general kind of likeness than the kind of likeness which exists between structures consisting of the same elements.

Because collocations and their items are less general than grammatical structures and their elements, they cannot be studied in quite the same way.

A greater amount of data is necessary to produce worthwhile results in a lexical study than in a study of grammatical structure. Because an element of structure is more general (can be realised by more items), than an individual item (which can be realised only by itself, though *realised* is perhaps the wrong term here), it can be found more frequently in a text. For instance, if a study were being made of the element predicator in a text, it would be a fair assumption that a predicator could be found in each of most of the clauses in the text. On the other hand, if a particular item, such as *spill,* were being studied, this item would certainly occur less frequently than the element predicator and might even occur only once or twice in the text. Thus in order to study a number of occurrences of the item comparable with the number of occurrences of the element, it would be necessary to study other texts in addition to the one text which would on its own yield worthwhile information about the element.

Because each element occurs more frequently than each item, a native speaker of a language has a greater experience, conscious or subconscious, of the relationships which exist between two elements than of the relationships which exist between two items. For this reason a linguist studying grammatical structure can rely more on his own intuitions than can a linguist studying collocations. Consequently linguists studying collocations resort more quickly to the use of statistical techniques in order to obtain more objective verification of their observations.

The relationships between the items of a collocation are, in fact, usually expressed in terms of statistical probability. The relationship between any two items is the probability (that is, the greatness of the likelihood) that one item will occur with the other. Some pairs of items have a strong probability of co-occurrence relationship, while other pairs have a weak probability of co-occurrence relationship. There is a greater likelihood, for instance, that *cat* will occur with *scratch* than that *cat* will occur with *music. cat* and *scratch* have a relatively strong probability of co-occurrence relationship, while *cat* and *music* have a relatively weak probability of co-occurrence relationship.

The strength of the probability of co-occurrence relationship between a pair of items can be measured by comparing the number of times that the two items occur together, with the total number of times that each of the items occurs. *cat* and *scratch* will occur together quite a large number of times in proportion to the total number of times that *cat* occurs and in proportion to the total number of times that *scratch* occurs. *cat* and *music* will occur together only a small number of times in proportion to the total number of times that each of the items occurs. *the* and *cat* might at first sight seem to have a strong probability of co-occurrence relationship, since they do often occur together. But when the number of times they occur together is compared with the total number of times that *the* occurs, they are found to have a relatively weak probability of co-occurrence relationship. The more times a particular item occurs, the less significant is its co-occurrence with any other particular item, unless it can be shown to co-occur with that item a very high proportion of the total number of times on which it occurs.

Some pairs of items have such a weak probability of co-occurrence relationship that it is unprofitable to pursue the relationship between them. They can be considered irrelevant to each other from a lexical point of view.

Another problem which arises from the lack of generality of collocations and their items is the question of knowing where to begin. Elements of structure can be compared with each other on the basis of shared or not shared properties and focal points of interest arise from the comparison. For instance, if one is considering the structure of the nominal group, the obvious focal point of interest is the headword. Modifiers and qualifiers can be considered in relation to the headword. On the other hand, if one is considering a collocation, there is no natural focal point, no natural headword. There is no reason why any one of the items of the collocation

The waitress spilt the soup on the tablecloth

should be regarded as a headword any more than any of the others. The items are unique and cannot be compared.

This problem is usually solved by the artificial creation of a 'headword'. An item is selected on which interest is to be focussed. This item temporarily becomes the 'headword' and the other items in the collocation are considered in relation to the selected item. The grounds on which the selection is made are usually not lexical grounds at all. One might, for instance, have a grammatical reason for the selection; one might be interested in the items which realise the element headword of nominal groups which act as the subjects of clauses. In this case one would choose *waitress* as the 'headword' of the above collocation. Alternatively one might have a contextual reason; one might be interested in items which realise food concepts. In this case one would choose *soup*. These artificial 'headwords' are called **nodes**. The items which occur with a node in a collocation are called the **collocates** of the node. If *waitress* was chosen as the node of the above collocation, *soup* would be one of its collocates. If *soup* were chosen as the node, *waitress* would be one of its collocates.

(In an ideal lexical study every item in turn would be treated as the node. For all the vast number of items which occur in a worthwhile amount of data to be treated in this way, the assistance of a computer is essential. Often one has to make do with a less than ideal lexical study.)

The strength of the probability of co-occurrence relationship between two items varies according to which of the items is being treated as the node and which the collocate. *cat* occurs with *the* more times in proportion to the total number of occurrences of *cat* than *the* occurs with *cat* in proportion to the total number of occurrences of *the*. If *cat* is the node, the relationship is stronger than if *the* is the node.

A collocation, then, can be said to consist of a node and its collocates. It is important however to recognise that 'consists of' has a different implication here from the implication it has in the statement that the structure of a nominal group consists of the elements modifier, headword and qualifier. This latter statement represents a 'truth' about the English Language. The statement that a collocation consists of a node and its collocates simply refers to a convenient way in which a linguist organises his data.

3.2 UNITS

So far this chapter has been mainly concerned with the patterns of lexis. As was shown in the chapters on grammar, the stretches of language which act as the bits of a level's patterns and the stretches of language which carry the level's patterns are the units of that level.

The units which act as the bits of the patterns of lexis are called simply **lexical items**.

A lexical item is identified by its collocates; that is, one knows that a particular lexical item is a particular unique lexical item different from all other lexical items, because the list of items with which it can be collocated differs from the lists of items with which other items can be collocated. No two lexical items will have exactly the same list of possible collocates, though of course their lists may well have some items in common. The following utterances show three lexical items, *cat*, *dog* and *cats and dogs*, each occurring with some of its possible collocates.

Cats purr when happy and wave their tails when angry, but dogs wag their tails when happy and growl when angry.
If you don't want to get wet, you'd better take your umbrella because it's raining cats and dogs.

These three lexical items can be differentiated from each other on the basis of their collocates and can be shown to be three distinct lexical items. *Cat* is one lexical item. Its collocates include *purr, happy, wave, tail, angry*. *dog* is another lexical item. Its list of collocates has some items in common with *cat*'s list of collocates — for example, *tail, happy, angry* — but the list also includes some items which differentiate *dog* from *cat* — for example *wag, growl. cats and dogs* is a third lexical item quite distinct from the other two as is shown by the way in which its list of collocates differs from the lists of the other two. The collocates of *cats and dogs* include *wet, umbrella, rain.*

The distinct lexical item *cats and dogs,* as in the second of the utterances cited above, should be distinguished from *cat s* and *dog s,* as in an extended version of the first of the two utterances cited above.

Cats and dogs show their emotions in very different ways: cats purr when happy and wave their tails when angry, but dogs wag their tails when happy and growl when angry.

In this extended version of the first utterance, *cat* is the lexical item *cat* and *dog* is the lexical item *dog* in the first part of the utterance, just as in the second part of the utterance. Although the items *purr, tail, wag, growl* etc. occur in the second part of the utterance, they are just as much collocates of the first occurrence of *cat* and the first occurrence of *dog* as they are of the second occurrence of each. This utterance, both in its original form and in its extended form, has none of the items such as *wet, rain, umbrella* which are the distinguishing collocates of the lexical item *cats and dogs.*

As was implied earlier in the chapter, lexical items are the formal items of grammar considered from a different point of view. Lexical items are formal items considered as individual items. Grammatical formal items are formal items considered from the point of view of the elements of structure which they realise. Any lexical item is also a grammatical item. In the utterance

The waitress spilt the soup on the tablecloth

spill is a lexical item with a distinctive list of collocates, some of which are occurring with it here in this utterance. *spill* is also a grammatical item, here realising the element base of the structure of a word which is acting as the verb of a group which is acting as the predicator of the clause. *soup* too is a lexical item with a distinctive list of collocates, some of which are occurring with it here in this utterance. *soup* is also a grammatical item, here realising the element base of the structure of a word and the element headword of the structure of a group which is acting as the complement of the clause.

The correspondence between lexical items and grammatical items is not always a one-to-one correspondence. Any lexical item will always be a grammatical item but it will not always, every time it occurs, be the same grammatical item. In the utterances

I have read the first fifty pages of that book
Read the first fifty pages of that book
That book is very readable
Will readers of this book please refrain from turning down the corners

read is both a lexical item and a grammatical item each time it occurs. It is the same lexical item each time it occurs. On each occasion it has with it at least one of its distinctive collocates — *book*. However it is a different grammatical item each time it occurs. It is true that the four grammatical items which *read* represents in these utterances have in common that they are all realising the element base of the structure of a word, but they can be differentiated by reference to the part the word in question is playing in the structure of a group and by reference to the terms from systems which the word is directly or indirectly realising or helping to realise. A number of different grammatical items can thus correspond to one lexical item. A list of grammatical items which correspond to a lexical item is called the lexical item's **scatter**. The scatter of the lexical item *read* includes *read, read(er), read(able)*. Similarly the scatter of the lexical item *strong* includes *strong, streng(th), strong(ly)*.

Lexical items, then, are also grammatical items but there is not necessarily a one-to-one correspondence between a particular lexical item and a particular grammatical item.

There must theoretically be at least one other unit of lexis in addition to the lexical item. As was shown in the chapters on grammar, not only is a pattern made up of stretches of language which are members of a unit; it is also carried by a stretch of language, which is a member of a higher unit. The mhq kind of structure, for instance, is made up of stretches of language which are members of the word. It is carried by a stretch of language which is a member of a higher unit, the group. The SPCA kind of structure is made up of stretches of language which are members of the group. It is carried by a stretch of language which is a member of a higher unit, the clause. In lexis a collocation is made up of stretches of language which are members of the lexical item. What are the stretches of language which carry collocations? Are they members of a higher unit? If so, how is this higher unit to be delimited? These are questions which have so far proved difficult to answer. Again we are up against the problem of the difficulty of making generalisations. The extent of the stretch of language which carries a collocation seems to vary according to what item we select as the node and according to what items we are distinguishing from the node. For instance, if we are trying to distinguish the lexical item *cats and dogs* as in

If you don't want to get wet, you'd better take your umbrella, because it's raining cats and dogs.

from the lexical item *cat* as in

Cats and dogs show their emotions in very different ways: cats purr when happy and wave their tails when angry, but dogs wag their tails when happy and growl when angry

the stretch of language which carries the relevant collocation for *cat* is the whole of the utterance *Cats and dogs... growl when angry*. On the other hand, if we are trying to distinguish the lexical item *cat* from the lexical item *dog* in the utterance *Cats and dogs... growl when angry,* the stretch of language which carries the relevant collocation for *cat* is *cats purr when happy and wave their tails when angry*. It is very difficult, in fact, to tell where collocations begin and end.

Because it is so difficult to delimit collocations and the units which carry them, linguists studying lexis have had to limit in an artificial way the stretches of language they examine. They cannot decide to study clauses, for instance, or groups as grammarians can. They have to set up artificial units for themselves. For each lexical study a **span** is selected, to fix the extent of the stretches of language to be considered. If a span of one is chosen the stretches of language to be examined will each consist of the node and one lexical item on either side of the node. If a span of three is chosen, the stretches of language to be examined will each consist of the node and three lexical items on either side of it. Ideally a lexical study would consist of a number of smaller studies each with a different span, so that it could be seen whether the strength of the probability of co-occurrence relationship between two items varied according to the span chosen.

3.3 RANK

Since there is only one unit which can be delimited with any degree of confidence, it is difficult to apply the concept of rank to lexis, though

theoretically there must be a rank scale, with the lexical item as the lowest
unit and with a higher unit which consists of lexical items.

Although both grammar and lexis, at least in theory, have a rank scale,
there is no regular correspondence between the scales of the two levels. It
is impossible to equate a point on one of the scales with a point on the
other.

It is impossible to equate the lexical item with any one grammatical
unit. Sometimes lexical items are coextensive with formal items belonging
to the morpheme as in *spil(t)* and *read(er)*. Sometimes lexical items are
coextensive with formal items belonging to the word, as in *soup* and
umbrella. Sometimes lexical items are coextensive with formal items
belonging to the group as in *cats and dogs*. Sometimes lexical items are
coextensive with formal items belonging to even higher grammatical units.
Burn the candle at both ends, for instance, could be regarded as a lexical
item. It would be likely to have as its collocates lexical items such as *tired,
unwise, nervous breakdown* and these would distinguish it from lexical
items such as *burn, candle* and *end* used separately. In the utterance

*Burn the candle at both ends and you will be too tired to work
efficiently*

Burn the candle at both ends is coextensive with a formal item acting as a
clause. The above examples show that lexical items vary as to the rank of
grammatical unit with which they are coextensive. They need not, in fact,
be coextensive with any grammatical unit. In

*He has been burning the candle at both ends for some time now and as
a result has had a nervous breakdown*

burn the candle at both ends is more than a group but less than a clause.
The lexical item, then, the lowest point on the rank scale of lexis, does
not regularly correspond with any unit on the rank scale of grammar.

It does not seem likely that the higher unit of lexis either, if it is ever
possible to delimit a higher unit, will regularly correspond with any
grammatical unit.

The most that can be said about any correspondence between the rank
scale of grammar and the rank scale of lexis is that there is a tendency for
the lexical item to be more frequently coextensive with the lower units of
grammar than with the higher units of grammar, and that there is likely to
be a tendency for the higher unit of lexis to be more frequently coextensive
with the higher units of grammar than with the lower units of grammar.

3.4 CLUSTERS AND SETS

Lexical items can be divided into **clusters** and **sets**, which are in some ways analogous to the classes of grammar.

A cluster is a list of the lexical items which can be collocated with a particular lexical item. Each node has its own cluster. *cats and dogs,* for instance, has a cluster which includes the items *rain, wet, umbrella. dog* has a cluster which includes the items *wag, growl, tail.* All the possible collocates of a node belong to its cluster. As was pointed out earlier in the chapter, it is by means of its potential collocates, its cluster, that a part- icular lexical item can be identified as a distinct lexical item and it is by means of selected members of its cluster, those actually occurring with it in a collocation, that a particular lexical item can be recognised when it occurs in a particular utterance.

A cluster is to a collocation as a grammatical class is to a grammatical structure. A cluster, like a grammatical class, is a list of things from which we choose in order to fill a place in a pattern. We choose an item from a class in order to fill a place in a structure. We choose an item from a cluster in order to fill a place in a collocation.

Sets are to lexical clusters as cross-classes are to grammatical classes. If a number of clusters are alike in that they have a large number of items in common, they can be conflated to form a set. The nodes of such clusters will usually be found in each other's clusters. The collocates of each node will have a strong probability of co-occurrence relationship with each other as well as with the node. The cluster of the item *cat* includes the items *mew, piteous, purr, contented, tail, fur, milk, lap.* The cluster of the item *mew* includes the items *cat, piteous, purr, contented, tail, fur, milk, lap.* The cluster of the item *purr* includes the items *cat, mew, piteous, contented, tail, fur, milk, lap.* These clusters have a large number of items in common. The node of each cluster is included in the clusters of the other two nodes. The collocates of each node have a strong probability of co-occurrence relationship with each other. These clusters can be conflated and can be described as a lexical set.

3.5 SYSTEMS

In Sections 3.1, 2 and 3 we were concerned with the surface things of lexis in relation to the axis of chain. In Section 3.4 we shifted the focus of our attention from the axis of chain to the axis of choice. However we were still concerned with the surface things of lexis. It was the surface choices

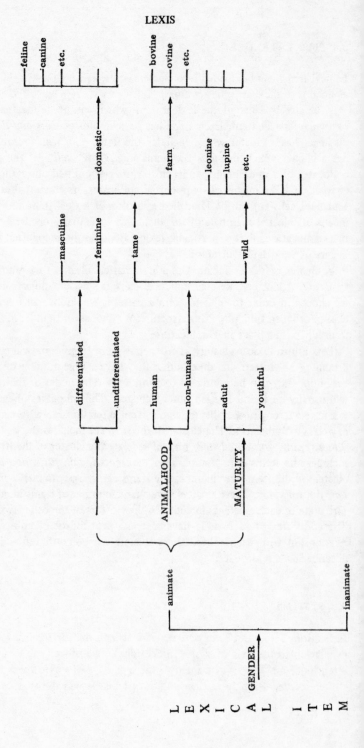

FIGURE 3.1

Network of gender systems etc.

of lexis that we were considering in Section 3.4 rather than the more fundamental choices. In this section we shall be considering the more fundamental choices of lexis, the meaning choices.

We saw in the grammar chapters of this book that grammatical units have meanings, the meaning of each unit being a composite meaning consisting of a number of features, the terms which the unit has chosen from systems. The meaning of the clause

The cow jumped over the moon

for example, includes the features major, material process, action process, intention process, restricted process, middle, unmarked theme, indicative, declarative, modality neutral.

Lexical units too have meanings. As in grammar the meaning of each unit is a composite meaning consisting of a number of features, the terms which the unit has chosen from systems. The meaning of the lexical item *cow* for instance includes the features bovine, feminine and adult. The meaning of the lexical item *bull* includes the features bovine, masculine and adult. The meaning of the lexical item *heifer* includes the features bovine, feminine and not adult. The meaning of the lexical item *calf* includes the features bovine, undifferentiated and not adult. The meaning of the lexical item *lamb* includes the features ovine, undifferentiated and not adult.

The systems from which lexical units choose can, like grammatical systems, be codified in networks.

If, for instance, we were trying to devise a network for the systems which provide the features for the lexical items discussed above (together with other items of the same and similar sets), we should probably arrive at something like the network shown in Figure 3.1.

Similarly, if we were trying to devise a network for the systems which provide the features for items such as *hot, warm, cool, cold*, we should probably arrive at something like the following.

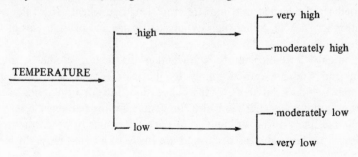

The items *hot* and *warm* have both chosen high from this network in contrast with the items *cool* and *cold* which have both chosen low. The item *hot* has gone on to choose very high in contrast with the item *warm* which has chosen moderately high. The item *cool* has chosen moderately low in contrast with the item *cold* which has chosen very low.

As we have seen, the item *cool* has chosen low and moderately low from the above network. The item *chilly* has also chosen low and moderately low from this network. If we want to distinguish between the meanings of these two items we shall have to add another system to our network:

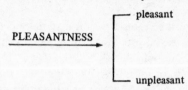

The meaning of the item *cool,* as in the advertising phrase *the refreshing cool of Cola,* includes the features low, moderately low and pleasant. The meaning of the item *chilly,* as in *It's a bit chilly today, isn't it?,* includes the features low, moderately low and unpleasant. The two items are alike in the features which they have chosen from the temperature systems but differ in the features they have chosen from the pleasantness system.

It is not always easy to tell whether a system has as its point of origin the lower lexical unit or the higher lexical unit.

In the utterance

The cat purred contentedly

the feature feline can certainly be said to belong to the lexical item *cat;* it can almost certainly be said to belong to the lexical item *purr;* it can possibly be said to belong to the lexical item *content,* since cats and contentment are often associated with each other. Since it seems to belong to more than one of the lexical items, it should perhaps be said to be carried by the higher unit, the stretch of language which carries the collocation as a whole, rather than by any particular one of the items in the collocation.

Similarly it is difficult to say whether the features domestic, farm, tame and wild are carried simply by the lexical items referring to the animals in these classes or by the collocations in which the items occur. Certainly the collocations in which the items referring to domestic animals occur are likely to be different from the collocations in which the items referring to farm animals occur and are likely to be even more different from the collocations in which the items referring to wild animals occur. We all know that the *cat* sat on the *mat*. A *dog* too might well sit on a *mat*. We are unlikely to hear of a *horse* or a *cow* sitting on a *mat*, still less a *giraffe* or a *gazelle*.

Nor is it easy to tell whether a feature is realised by the lower lexical unit or by the higher lexical unit.

The fact that even if we have never met a particular item before we are often able to deduce quite a lot about its meaning simply from looking at its collocates suggests that some of the features of its meaning are realised by the whole collocation rather than by the individual item. Anyone looking at the stretch of language

The ripe and luscious boobles tasted delicious

is unlikely ever to have seen the item *boobles* before since I have just made it up. They will not know exactly what I intended it to mean. However they will be able to deduce something about its meaning from looking at its collocates. They will be able to deduce that its meaning includes the feature eatable and more specifically the feature fruit.

It is not as easy in lexis as in grammar, then, to assign a particular feature to a particular size of stretch of language.

The uncertainty shown in the previous few paragraphs may be partly due simply to the fact that not as much work has been carried out on lexis within the framework of the systemic model of language as has been carried out on grammar. We are not as experienced at handling lexical meanings and forms and relating the two to each other as we are at handling grammatical meanings and forms and their relationships.

The problem is probably not just a matter of inexperience however. We are probably up against another difficulty resulting from the differing natures of grammar and lexis. We saw earlier in the chapter that it was difficult to make generalisations about lexical items and collocations because each was unique, and important because it was unique rather than because of any properties which it shared with other items or collocations. We are probably up against a similar difficulty here.

In grammar there is a regularity about the size, or rather status, of the stretches of language which are affected by (i.e. which choose or realise) each particular feature. It is possible to predict with a reasonable degree of certainty that the stretches of language affected by a given feature will be of a particular size or status, no more, no less. It is possible to predict for instance that the stretch of language affected by the feature imperative will be a clause — an α clause. As soon as another α clause comes along a new and quite independent choice from the mood system will be made.

In lexis there is no such regularity and therefore no such predictability. The feature feline, for example, may affect just a single item, or a short collocation as a whole, or a long collocation as a whole. Once one begins talking about a cat one's choice of lexical items is limited to those which have something to do with a cat. If one wishes to express the meaning 'make a noise of pleasure' one virtually has, if one is talking about a cat, to use the lexical item *purr*. If one wishes to refer to the covering that grows on a cat's skin, one virtually has to use the item *fur* rather than the item *hair*. One is not free to make a new and indepandent choice, to choose from a different set of lexical items, until one stops talking about a cat. It is impossible to predict in formal terms the extent of the stretch of language over which this influence of the feature feline will operate. All one can say is that the feature feline will extend until the speaker or writer stops referring to a cat and starts referring to something else. Each occurrence of the feature feline affects a different size of stretch of language. It is very difficult to make generalisations or predictions.

We have seen then that the systems of lexis differ from the systems of grammar in the regularity and predictability with which they affect different sizes of formal item. The systems of the two levels differ in the way in which they influence the form.

Do the systems of the two levels differ in themselves? Is there any way in which the systems of lexis are inherently different from the systems of grammar?

One way in which it has been suggested that the systems of the two levels differ is that the systems of lexis are 'less finite' than the systems of grammar.

We certainly had no difficulty in deciding in Chapter 8 of Volume 1 that the systems of grammar were finite. We do have some difficulty in deciding whether some of the systems of lexis are finite. For instance it is difficult to decide whether the system leonine/lupine/etc. is finite. This system is certainly not infinite. (The only system which is genuinely infinite is the numeral system which is carried by the lexical items *one, two, three,* etc.) But it is so large as not to be really countable. On the other hand the lexical system wild/tame is easily countable and certainly finite.

Here again we must admit that insufficient work has been carried out on the systems of lexis. It may well be that it is simply because they have not been so well worked out that some lexical systems seem 'less finite' than grammatical systems. It may well be that eventually, by dividing and subdividing the terms in the system of wild animals, we shall arrive at a series of systems which are indubitably finite. On the other hand it may be that some systems are genuinely less countable than others. If so it may well be that there is a tendency for lexical systems to be among the less countable while grammatical systems are among the more countable.

In this respect the systems of the two levels would appear, if they differ at all, to differ in degree rather than in kind, the two levels being related on a cline. (As explained in Section 2.1.4 of Volume 1, a cline is a scale on which there are no discrete points. The stages on the scale shade into each other so that it is impossible to say where one stage ends and the next begins.)

Another suggestion as to a way in which the systems of the two levels may differ is that features from lexical systems are rarer than those from grammatical systems, that lexical systems are less frequently chosen from than grammatical systems.

We make a choice from the grammatical system major/minor every time we speak. We only occasionally make a choice from the lexical system leonine/lupine/etc. Again however this is not equally true of all the systems which we have treated in this section as lexical systems. The systems masculine/feminine and differentiated/undifferentiated are very frequently chosen from, the system animate/inanimate even more so.

Again this appears to be a tendency rather than a hard and fast rule, a difference in degree rather than a difference in kind. Again the two levels appear to be related on a cline.

3.6 DELICACY

We can certainly say that the systems of lexis, like the systems of grammar, are ordered in delicacy.

For instance the system feline/canine/etc. is more delicate than the system domestic/farm which in turn is more delicate than the system tame/wild.

Let us now return to something less certain, the question of the exact relationship between the systems of lexis and the systems of grammar.

It has been suggested that the cline on which the systems of lexis and the systems of grammar are related is really the scale of delicacy, lexical systems being simply more delicate grammatical systems.

This seems a very plausible suggestion.

It is very difficult to tell whether some systems are grammatical systems or lexical systems since they seem to be related on the scale of delicacy both to more certainly grammatical systems and to more certainly lexical systems. The system animate/inanimate, for instance, as we saw in Chapter

8 of Volume 1 is very closely related to the grammatical transitivity systems. The system animate/inanimate is also at the grammatical end of the countability cline and the frequency of choice cline referred to in the previous section of the present chapter. On these grounds the animate/ inanimate system would appear to be a grammatical system. However this system is also related on the scale of delicacy to the lexical systems leonine/lupine/etc. and feline/canine/etc. since a choice from either of these systems depends on animate having been chosen in preference to inanimate. It does seem as if one scale of delicacy relates all grammatical systems and all lexical systems, the point at which grammatical systems shade into lexical systems being indeterminate.

The suggestion that lexical systems are more delicate than grammatical systems would seem to tie up with the suggestion that lexical systems are less frequently chosen from than grammatical systems. If terms in lexical systems are subdivisions of the semantic categories which act as the terms in grammatical systems, it is only to be expected that each should occur less frequently than the more general category of which it is a sub-category.

It would seem then that it is not possible to make a sharp distinction between grammatical systems and lexical systems on the basis of the nature of the systems themselves. If a distinction is to be made between the systems of lexis and the systems of grammar it must be on the basis of the way in which each relates to linguistic form.

3.7 REALISATION

3.7.1 *Realisation within Lexis*

We have seen that lexis, like grammar, has surface things — formal items and patterns — and more fundamental things — meanings. In lexis, as in grammar, the more fundamental things are realised by the surface things.

In grammar the formal contrasts which realise the meaning contrasts take the form of contrasts between different structures and contrasts between classes and sub-classes of formal items.

In lexis, the formal contrasts are provided by the formal items themselves, not this time as members of classes, but as individual unique items.

man contrasts with *woman, bull* contrasts with *cow, ram* contrasts with *ewe,* and thus *man, bull* and *ram* are able to realise the feature masculine, distinguishing it from the feature feminine which is realised by *woman, cow* and *ewe. cow* contrasts with *ewe, sow* and *mare,* and *bull* contrasts with *ram, boar* and *stallion,* and thus *cow* and *bull* are able to realise the feature bovine, distinguishing it from the features ovine, porcine and equine which are realised respectively by *ewe* and *ram, sow* and *boar, mare* and *stallion.*

The realisation statements of lexis are rather like the particularisation realisation statements of grammar. Like the particularisation realisation statements of grammar, the realisation statements of lexis narrow the choice of formal item.

However the realisation statements of lexis differ from the particularisation realisation statements of grammar in two main ways.

The realisation statements of lexis narrow the choice of formal item further than the particularisation realisation statements of grammar. The particularisation realisation statements of grammar only narrow the choice of formal item to a particular class or sub-class. The realisation statements of lexis narrow the choice of formal item to a particular individual unique item.

Secondly, whereas the realisation statements of grammar tend to be attached to single features, the realisation statements of lexis tend to be attached to combinations of features. In grammar one says: If mental process is chosen, select an item from the mental sub-class of verbal groups. In lexis one does not say: If feminine is chosen, select the item *cow;* if masculine is chosen, select the item *ram.* One says: If feminine and adult and bovine are chosen, select the item *cow;* if masculine and adult and ovine are chosen, select the item *ram.*

These differences between the realisation processes of lexis and the realisation processes of grammar could again be regarded as differences in degree rather than differences in kind.

It could be argued that particularisation is really a continuous process beginning in grammar and ending in lexis, gradually narrowing the choice of formal item through member of a unit, member of a class, member of a sub-class, member of a sub-sub-class etc., to member of a one-member class, i.e. to the individual unique formal item. The particularisation realisation statements of lexis would then be simply more particular grammatical particularisation realisation statements. The realisation processes of lexis would then be related to the realisation processes of grammar on a cline of particularisation, this cline being actually part of the scale of realisation.

The second difference between the two levels could be regarded as following from the first. The further one moves along the scale of realisation the greater number of previous decisions one is likely to have to take into account. If we took a cross-section of the grammatical part of the particularisation stage of the realisation scale we should find that there is already evidence of cross-classification rather than just a single process of sub-classification. For instance if we were concerned with the particularisation moves specified by terms from some of the transitivity systems we should find that simultaneously with a process of sub-classification specified by terms from the systems relating to type of process there is a process of sub-classification specified by terms from systems relating to number of participant roles. At one point on the scale there is sub-classification specified by the choice from the action process/event process system and also sub-classification specified by the choice from the restricted process/ unrestricted process system. These two kinds of sub-classification cut across each other. The limiting of the choice of formal item is the result of the interaction of these two kinds of sub-classification.

3.7.2 *The Realisation of Lexis by Phonology and Graphology*

Lexical items themselves are realised by sequences of phonological or graphological items. The fact that *cat, soup* and *rain* are different lexical items is made evident by the fact that they are realised by different sequences of phonological items and graphological items; *cat, soup* and *rain* sound different and look different.

Phonology and graphology do not always distinguish between different lexical items. *lean* meaning 'thin' and *lean* meaning 'bend over' are two distinct lexical items, as is clear from the fact that they have different clusters, but they are both realised by the same sequence of phonological items and the same sequence of graphological items. *refuse* meaning 'say no' and *refuse* meaning 'rubbish' are two distinct lexical items, as is clear from the fact that they have different clusters; these items are realised by different sequences of phonological items, but the same sequence of graphological items. *place* and *plaice* are two distinct lexical items, as is clear from the fact that they have different clusters; these items are realised by different sequences of graphological items, but the same sequence of phonological items. Thus two or more lexical items can be realised by the same sequence of phonological items and/or the same sequence of graphological items.

In cases such as these, where there is phonological and/or graphological ambiguity, it is the collocates of an item which enable us to recognise which item is intended when we meet it in a particular utterance.

3.8 DISCUSSION

3.8.1 *General Linguistics*

In Chapter 2 lexis was shown as being parallel with grammar on the scale of realisation. This implies something about the views of systemic linguists on the relationship between lexis and grammar (or at any rate it implies something about their views on the most convenient way of handling the internal and external relationships of lexis). It implies that they believe lexis and grammar are (or at any rate that they believe it is convenient to treat them as if they are) sufficiently different to be regarded as separate levels, yet sufficiently similar to be regarded as parallel levels.

That lexis and grammar are sufficiently different to be regarded as separate levels and that they are sufficiently similar to be treated as parallel levels are both open to question. Different views exist as to the exact relationship between lexis and grammar.

One view is that lexis is merely what is left over from grammar, that language should be described as far as possible in terms of grammar and that lexis should be resorted to only when grammar can go no further. This school of thought envisages the possibility of lexis eventually being subsumed under grammar. The more skilled linguists become at making detailed grammatical statements, the less need there will be for them to resort to lexical statements. If this process continues to its logical conclusion, lexis will eventually be swallowed up in grammar. This school of thought concedes that it is at present necessary, or at any rate convenient, to treat lexis and grammar as separate levels but considers that the necessity arises from the inexperience of linguists rather than from the nature of language.

Another view is that lexis and grammar are by their very nature different in kind. This school of thought believes that lexis will never be subsumed under grammar, that the two levels are distinct and always will be, that there is and always will be a need for lexical statements as well as grammatical statements.

Between these two extremes is a third view which is that lexis and grammar differ but differ only in degree, that there is no sharp division between lexis and grammar the two levels being related on a cline.

Let us reconsider some of the differences between lexis and grammar which we have noted in this chapter reminding ourselves whether they are differences which are likely to disappear altogether with further investigation, differences in degree, or differences in kind.

The differences between the systems of the two levels, the differences in countability, frequency of choice and delicacy, would appear to be either differences which will eventually disappear altogether or differences which are differences in degree (Sections 3.5 and 3.6).

The differences between the processes of realisation of the two levels, the differences in particularisation and number of features taken into account, would appear to be differences which are differences in degree (Section 3.7).

However the differences at the more surface end of the scale of realisation, the differences between the forms of the two levels, would appear to be differences which are differences in kind. We have seen that the units and patterns of lexis differ from the units and patterns of grammar in being less abstract, less generalised and therefore less general (Section 3.1). We have seen that the patterns of lexis differ from the patterns of grammar in being based only on co-occurrence rather than on position in sequence (Section 3.1). We have seen that the units of lexis are often not co-extensive with the units of grammar; the stretches of language affected by the systems of lexis are different stretches of language from those affected by the systems of grammar (Sections 3.2 and 3.3). We have seen that the stretches of language affected by the systems of lexis are less regular and predictable in their size or status than those affected by the systems of grammar (Section 3.5).

How far do these differences justify our treating lexis and grammar as separate levels?

Since the systems of the two levels and the realisation processes of the two levels appear to differ only in degree, it would be possible as far as these two aspects of language are concerned, to fuse lexis and grammar treating lexical systems simply as more delicate grammatical systems and lexical realisation statements simply as more particular grammatical particularisation realisation statements.

However there would appear to be sufficient difference between the forms of the two levels to warrant our treating them as separate levels. If we do not consider the patterns of lexis separately from the patterns of grammar, in the way suggested in the first two sections of this chapter, we are losing a perspective on language, a perspective which may be irrelevant for some purposes but which is highly desirable for other purposes.

Suppose then we agree that there is sufficient difference between lexis and grammar for them to be treated as separate levels. Do we also agree that the best way of representing any likeness between them is to place them in parallel positions on the realisation scale?

An alternative position for lexis would be as shown in Figure 3.2.

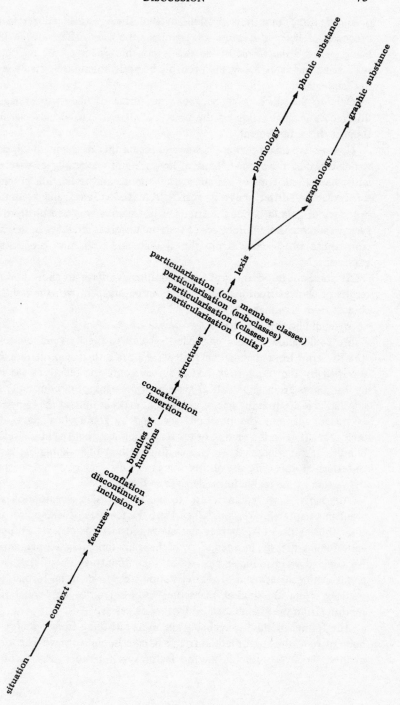

FIGURE 3.2 *An alternative view of the position of lexis on the realisation scale*

situation → context → features →

conflation
discontinuity
inclusion

bundles of
functions →

concatenation
insertion

structures →

particularisation (one member classes)
particularisation (sub-classes)
particularisation (classes)
particularisation (units)

lexis →

phonology → phonic substance

graphology → graphic substance

If we agree that it is possible to fuse the systems and realisation processes of lexis with those of grammar, the only differences in kind being between the forms of the two levels, the version of the realisation scale given in Figure 3.2 would probably be preferable to the version given in Chapter 2.

One of the differences between the forms of the two levels, the differences in abstraction of the units and patterns, would also seem to support this arrangement.

However we might perhaps hesitate to accept this arrangement when we remember that the formal items of lexis are not necessarily co-extensive with the formal items of grammar. The systems and realisation processes of lexis may differ only in degree from the systems and realisation processes of grammar, but the stretches of language which result from the systems and realisation processes of lexis are different stretches of language from those which result from the systems and realisation processes of grammar.

At some stage on the scale of realisation we have to show how the results of choices from lexical systems can be mapped onto the results of choices from grammatical systems.

We could do this in either of two ways.

We could allow terms from lexical systems to specify functions as we do with terms from grammatical systems. We could then map the functions specified by the terms from lexical systems onto the functions specified by the terms from grammatical systems, by means of discontinuity and conflation realisation statements at different ranks of unit, at the same time as we are mapping the functions specified by grammatical terms onto each other (i.e. on the section of the realisation scale between features and bundles of functions). If we choose this method of mapping the results of lexical choices onto the results of grammatical choices we are accepting the version of the realisation scale given in Figure 3.2.

Alternatively we could return to the version of the realisation scale given in Chapter 2. We could then treat the features of lexis as separate from the features of grammar and allow the features of lexis to specify lexical items directly, independently of the realisation processes of grammar. We could then introduce a new set of discontinuity and conflation statements at the surface end of the realisation scale to map the formal items resulting from the lexical realisation processes onto the formal items resulting from the grammatical realisation processes.

The former method is probably the more satisfying from a theoretical point of view, the latter method from a practical point of view. The former method would so complicate the features – functions section of the realisation scale that there would be a danger of not being able to see the wood for the trees.

Very little work has so far been carried out within the framework of the systemic model of language on ways of relating the results of lexical choices to the results of grammatical choices. As was said in Chapter 2, systemic linguistics is a multi-purpose approach to the study of language. For most of the purposes for which this kind of linguistics has so far been used the question of the exact relationship between lexis and grammar is largely irrelevant. The problem only arises in general linguistic studies primarily concerned with showing exactly how the surface forms of language are derived from the meanings.

3.8.2 *Descriptive Linguistics*

An interesting exercise in practical lexical description of English, though with the object of answering a number of theoretical questions, was carried out at Edinburgh and Birmingham between 1963 and 1969 under the direction of Professor J. McH. Sinclair (Sinclair et al. 1970).

3.8.3 *Contrastive Linguistics*

The lexis of two languages, or varieties of languages, may, like the grammar, differ semantically or formally or in the relationships between the meanings and the forms.

3.8.4 *Applied Linguistics*

Lexical study is of potential value to a number of kinds of applied linguistics. Perhaps particularly noteworthy here are: machine translation; information retrieval; stylistics, in which 'such concepts as the ability of a lexical item to "predict" its own environment, and the cohesive power of lexical relations, are of great potential interest'; and foreign language teaching, in which 'many errors are best explained collocationally, and items can be first introduced in their habitual environments'. (Professor Halliday, from whom the above quotations are taken, lists in a footnote examples of the kind of error he has in mind. Halliday 1966.)

One example may be given of an application of lexical study to literary study.

It was suggested in Section 3.5 that the extent of the stretch of language affected by a given feature varied irregularly and unpredictably from one occurrence to the next. It could perhaps be said that this variation is more carefully controlled in literary language than in most other registers.

For instance if we add a term to one of the gender systems and apply

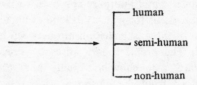

it to Richard Wilbur's poem *Beasts,* we find that the influence of the feature non-human extends over the first two stanzas, these two stanzas being dominated by the set of lexical items consistent with the choice of animate but non-human. Over the next two stanzas extends the influence of the feature semi-human, the key item here being *werewolf,* and the set of items consistent with the choice of non-human mingling with the set of items consistent with the choice of human. The feature human extends over the next stanza, appropriate lexical items being chosen. In the final stanza each lexical item appears to have made an independent choice from the system and items which have chosen human jostle with those which have chosen semi-human and non-human.

The patterning of the features and their appropriate lexical sets of course reflects the thought of the poem. A view of bestial nature in the first two stanzas is followed by a view of human nature in the next two stanzas, human nature being shown in many ways to resemble bestial nature. In the fifth stanza human nature is shown trying to rise above bestial nature. In the sixth stanza we are shown the chaos which results from the interference with bestial nature arising from the aspirations of human nature.

(It is perhaps worth noting that the first group of students with whom I discussed *Beasts* were having difficulty in determining its meaning; we found that a lexical analysis of the poem led to at least a partial understanding of the theme of the poem.)

3.8.5 *Systemic Linguistics and Other Schools of Linguistics*

Systemic linguistics perhaps attaches greater importance than some other schools to the need to study the patterns of lexis separately from the patterns of grammar.

4
Phonology

4.1 UNITS AND STRUCTURES

At the level of phonology, as at the levels of grammar and lexis, there are structures, which are the patterns along the axis of chain, and there are units, which are the stretches of language which carry the patterns and which make up the patterns.

The phonology of English is usually said to have four units: the **tone-group**, the **foot**, the **syllable** and the **phoneme**.

The tone-group is the unit which carries the intonation patterns, the pitch movements, of the language.

Each of the following utterances consists of a single tone-group; each has a single intonation pattern, a single pitch movement.

> Ex. 4.1 // *I've put the book on the table* //
> Ex. 4.2 // *The recital is at 7.30* //
> Ex. 4.3 // *Come when you can* //
> Ex. 4.4 //*What are you reading, Bill?* //

Each of the following utterances consists of two tone-groups; each has two separate intonation patterns, two separate pitch movements.

> Ex. 4.5 // *Don't put it there.* // *Put it on the table* //
> Ex. 4.6 // *When's the recital?* // *At 7.30?* //
> Ex. 4.7 // *When you leave the department,* // *please put out the light* //
> Ex. 4.8 // *What are you reading?* // *Shakespeare?* //

(A pair of oblique lines is the usual way of marking the boundary of a tone-group. Note that whereas vertical lines are used for the boundaries between grammatical units, oblique lines are used for the boundaries between phonological units.)

Since it is the highest phonological unit, the tone-group does not make up the structure of a higher unit. It does, however, have a structure of its own. The elements of this structure are the **tonic**, the **pre-tonic** and the **post-tonic**.

The tonic is the element which carries the main pitch movement of an intonation pattern. The most usual way of saying Ex. 4.1 would be to keep the pitch fairly level through *I've put the book on the* but to drop the pitch on the word *table*. *table* carries the main pitch movement of the intonation pattern. *table* is thus the tonic element of this particular tone-group. Similarly, the most usual way of saying Ex. 4.2 would be to keep the pitch fairly level through *The recital is at 7* but to drop the pitch on *30*. *30* carries the main pitch movement of the intonation pattern. *30* is the tonic element of the tone-group.

The tonic is the essential element of the structure of the tone-group. It is possible to have a tone-group which consists only of a tonic element. The second tone-group of Ex. 4.8, *//Shakespeare?//*, consists only of a tonic element. The intonation pattern consists just of a fairly marked upward pitch movement.

The pre-tonic element is the part of the tone-group which comes before the tonic. Thus in Ex. 4.1 the pre-tonic is *I've put the book on the* and in Ex. 4.2 the pre-tonic is *The recital is at 7*.

The post-tonic element is the part of the tone-group which comes after the tonic. In the tone-groups of most utterances, there is no post-tonic element. The most usual way of saying any utterance is to place the tonic at the end of its tone-group, as in the most usual way of saying Ex. 4.1 and Ex. 4.2 discussed above. However it is possible to say these utterances in a different way. One could, for example, emphasise the word *book* in Ex. 4.1, as if the utterance were in answer to the question *What did you say you've put on the table? book on the* would then be the tonic element of the tone-group. *I've put the* would be the pre-tonic. And there would be a post-tonic element, *table*.

> Not everyone would agree that there is such a thing as a post-tonic. an alternative analysis is to include in the tonic itself everything that comes after the main pitch movement.

The foot is the unit which carries the stress patterns of the language. Each of the following utterances consists of four feet.

Ex. 4.9   /Little Miss / Muffet / Sat on her / tuffet /
Ex. 4.10 /Thank you for / giving me such a / wonderful / time /
Ex. 4.11 /Come and / see me in my / office to- / morrow. /

Each of the following utterances consists of three feet.

Ex. 4.12 / What are you / reading, / Bill? /
Ex. 4.13 / Whose is the / book on the / table? /
Ex. 4.14 / Men have / landed on the / moon /

(A single oblique line is the usual way of marking the boundary of a foot.)

(The analysis given above of Ex. 4.9 to Ex. 4.14 is based on what is probably the most usual way of saying these utterances. It would be possible to say them in a different way and consequently to analyse them into feet in a different way. For instance, it would be possible to say Ex. 4.11 with emphasis on *me*. (*You didn't manage to see Miss Brown? O.K. Come and see me in my office to-morrow.*)

The example could then be analysed into feet thus:

Ex. 4.15 / *Come and see* / *me in my* / *office to-* / *morrow* /)

The structure of the foot consists of the elements **salient** and **weak.**

The salient element is the stressed part of the foot. In Ex. 4.10 *Thank* is the salient element of the first foot, *gi-* of the second foot, *won-* of the third foot and *time* of the fourth foot.

The salient element is the essential element of the structure of the foot. It is possible to have a foot which consists only of a salient element, as for example *time,* the fourth foot of Ex. 4.10.

The salient element is always at the beginning of the foot. It will be seen from this that the term *foot* is being used rather differently here from the way in which it is traditionally used in connection with metre. A linguistic foot, as opposed to a metrical foot, is more like a bar in music, which also has its strongest beat at the beginning.

The salient element may be silent.* Here again music may be cited as an analogy, since it is possible for a bar to begin with a rest. Each of the following utterances may be spoken in such a way that one of its feet has a silent salient element, a **silent beat,** as it is called.

Ex. 4.16 / *When's the re* / *cital?* / Λ *at* / *7* / *30?* /
Ex. 4.17 / *When you* / *leave the de* / *partment,* / Λ *will you* /
        please put / *out the* / *light?* /
Ex. 4.18 ... *thirty-* / *seven thirty-* / *eight thirty-* / *nine* / *forty* /
        Λ *forty-* / *one forty-* / *two forty-* / *three* ...

(The symbol Λ is the usual way of indicating a silent beat.) It is possible for a whole foot to be silent, if the foot consists only of a salient element and if that salient element is a silent beat. Ex. 4.8 could be spoken in such a way as to contain a silent foot.

Ex. 4.19 / *What are you* / *reading?* / Λ / *Shakespeare?* /

*Abercrombie, 1964

In phonology, silence is often as important as sound.

The weak element of the structure of the foot is the unstressed part of the foot. There may be more than one weak element in a foot. In

Ex. 4.11 / *Come and* / *see me in my* / *office to-* / *morrow* /

the first foot and the last foot each have one weak element, the third foot has two weak elements, and the second foot has three weak elements. In

Ex. 4.10 / *Thank you for* / *giving me such a* / *wonderful* / *time* /

the first foot and the third foot each have two weak elements, the second foot has four weak elements, while the last foot has no weak element.

As well as having a structure of its own, the foot provides the elements which make up the structure of the tone-group. The tonic element of a tone-group is a whole foot, while the pre-tonic and post-tonic elements each consist of one or more whole feet. Ex. 4.1 can be further analysed as

Ex. 4.20 // / Λ *I've* / *put the* / *book on the* / **table** / // or
Ex. 4.21 // / Λ *I've* / *put the* / **book on the** / *table* / //

according to whether the emphasis is on *table* or *book*. In Ex. 4.20 the tonic element is the foot *table,* which is preceded by a pre-tonic element consisting of three feet. In Ex. 4.21 the tonic element is the foot *book on the,* which is preceded by a pre-tonic element consisting of two feet and followed by a post-tonic element consisting of one foot.

The term used for the third phonological unit of English, *syllable,* will already be familiar. When used in linguistics this term has the same meaning as it has when used in everyday language.

The following stretches of language each consist of four syllables

Ex. 4.22   *pho no lo gy*
Ex. 4.23   *Come if you can*
Ex. 4.24   *Hea ven sa bove (Heavens above!)*

(The usual way of indicating the boundary between two syllables is by leaving a space between them.)

The structure of the syllable consists of the elements **vowel** and **consonant.** These terms also mean the same as they do in everyday language. (Though readers are warned against a common layman's error, which is to assume that these terms refer to letters whereas in fact they refer to sounds.)

Examples of syllables analysed into their structures are the following:

Ex. 4.25   *strap* – C C C V C
Ex. 4.26   *bends* – C V C C C
Ex. 4.27   *trips* – C C V C C
Ex. 4.28   *rock* – C V C
Ex. 4.29   *the* – C V
Ex. 4.30   *am* – V C
Ex. 4.31   *I* – V

(The letter C is used to symbolise the element consonant, the letter V to symbolise the element vowel.)

The vowel is the essential element of the structure of a syllable; every syllable must have a vowel. Each syllable has only one vowel.

The consonant is a non-essential element. Example 4.31, for instance, has no consonant. A syllable may have up to three consonants before its vowel and up to three consonants after its vowel.

As well as having a structure of its own, the syllable provides the elements which make up the structure of a foot. For instance each element of the foot

/ *gi ving me such a* /

is a syllable, there being five syllables in the foot, one acting as the salient element and the others acting as weak elements.

Phonemes are what are usually thought of as being the individual sounds of the language.

p, b, t, d, k, for instance, are phonemes of English. (Again it should be emphasised that we are talking about sounds, not letters.)

Being the smallest phonological unit, the phoneme has no structure. It does however provide the elements which make up the structure of the syllable. The structure of the syllable *trips,* for instance, consists of five elements, as shown above. Each element is a phoneme. The syllable consists of five phonemes. Similarly the structure of the syllable *rock* consists of three elements, as shown above. Again each element is a phoneme. The syllable consists of three phonemes

No phonological unit of a language can be automatically equated with any grammatical unit or any lexical unit of the language.

In English it frequently happens that a stretch of language which is a phonological tone-group is also a grammatical clause. In Ex. 4.7, for instance,

‖ // *When you leave the department,* ‖ // *please put out the light* // ‖

each of the two tone-groups is also a clause. But this is by no means always the case. In the following example

Ex. 4.32   ‖ // *In August* // *, the halfpenny will be going out of use* // ‖

there are two tone-groups but only one clause, and in Ex. 4.3

‖ // *Come* ‖ *when you can* // ‖

there are two clauses but only one tone-group.

Similarly, a stretch of language which is a phonological syllable is frequently also a grammatical morpheme, as in

Ex. 4.33 $^+do^+ing^+$
Ex. 4.34 $^+un^+clean^+$

But again this is by no means always the case.

Ex. 4.35 $^+Au\ gust^+$

is two syllables but only one morpheme.

Ex. 4.36 $^+I^{+}m^+$

is two morphemes but only one syllable.

Ex. 4.37 $^+squi\ rrel^+s^+$

is both two syllables and two morphemes but the syllable boundary comes in a different place from the morpheme boundary.

4.2 RANK

The phonological units can be arranged on a rank scale in the same way as the grammatical units.

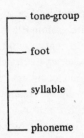

tone-group

foot

syllable

phoneme

A tone-group consists of one or more feet. A foot consists of one or more syllables. A syllable consists of one or more phonemes.

There is no possibility of rankshift for the units on the phonological rank scale. A tone-group, for instance, always functions as a tone-group, never as a foot or a syllable. In this respect a tone-group can be contrasted with a grammatical unit such as a clause, which, as was explained in Chapter 7 of Volume 1, can sometimes function as a group or a word.

The reason why phonological units, unlike grammatical units, cannot be rankshifted is that phonological units are not so like each other as grammatical units. Both phonological and grammatical units are formed on the basis of the patterns which they carry. All grammatical units carry the same kind of pattern—patterns consisting of certain classes of item occurring in certain sequences. Phonological units carry different kinds of pattern: tone-groups carry patterns of pitch; feet carry patterns of stress; syllables carry patterns of differently articulated sounds. Grammatical units are so like each other as to be able to be substituted for each other on occasion. Phonological units can never be substituted for each other since the substitution would involve not only a change of rank but also a change of kind.

4.3 SYSTEMS

In phonology, as in grammar and lexis, there are formal choices or contrasts which assist in the realisation of meanings. We shall first consider some of these formal contrasts, noting the meaning contrasts which underlie them: We shall then consider how some of the meaning contrasts underlying the formal contrasts can be codified in systems.

There are three sets of choices relating to the tone-group.

One set of choices relates to the location of tone-group boundaries.

We assume as a norm here that tone-group boundaries coincide with the clause boundaries of grammar. Whenever we speak we split up our message into **information units**; that is, we split it up into points to be noted. As a general rule each point is allocated a tone-group at the phonological level and a clause at the grammatical level. Both tone-groups and clauses are associated with information units, so we should expect the boundaries of tone-groups and clauses to coincide.

However tone-groups are more closely associated with information units than clauses are. Tone-groups always realise information units. Clauses usually do. Tone-groups and information units could almost be regarded as the same thing except that the tone-group is a formal category whereas the information unit is a meaning category. Certainly tone-groups and information units always coincide, the one realising the other; any stretch of language which carries a tone-group also carries an information unit, the tone-group indicating the presence of the information unit. The clause and the information unit on the other hand are independent variables. Usually a stretch of language which is a clause is carrying an information unit, but not necessarily so,

We do in fact have a choice when we speak between an unmarked (most usual) distribution of tone-groups and information units, one tone-group and information unit per clause, and a marked (less usual) distribution, anything other than one tone-group and information unit per clause. We could say

Ex. 4.38 // ‖ *On Wednesday Dr Brown is giving a talk to the Mothers' Union* ‖ //

Here we do have the most normal distribution of one tone-group to one clause. We have made the clause equal one information unit. Or we could say

Ex. 4.39 // ‖ *On Wednesday* // *Dr Brown is giving a talk to the Mothers' Union* ‖ //

The utterance is still a single clause but it is now two tone-groups. We have made it into two information units. There are now two points to be particularly noted: the fact that Dr Brown is giving a talk to the Mothers' Union; and the fact that this is happening on Wednesday. Or we could say

Ex. 4.40 // ‖ *On Wednesday* // *Dr Brown is giving a talk* // *to the Mothers' Union* ‖ //

The utterance is still a single clause, but now three tone-groups, three information units. There are now three points to be particularly noted: the fact that Dr Brown is giving a talk; the fact that it is happening on

Wednesday; and the fact that the talk is to the Mothers' Union. We could carry this to extremes and make every single word a separate tone-group

Ex. 4.41 // || *On* // *Wednesday* // *Dr* // *Brown* // *is* // *giving* // *a* // *talk* // *to* // *the* // *Mothers'* // *Union* || //

This would seem to be what novelists mean when they write of their characters 'speaking in capitals'.

The possible reasons for our choosing to assign more than one tone-group, and therefore more than one information unit, to a clause are many and various. It may be that the message itself is particularly important so that it is particularly necessary to make sure that every bit of it is clear. It may be that the message contains a lot of new information so that the hearer cannot guess any of it from the context or from what he knows already. It may be that there is something in the immediate situation of the utterance which makes communication difficult, such as a bad line on the telephone. It may be that the speaker is a long way away from the hearer. It may be that the speaker knows the hearer to be rather deaf or even that the speaker thinks the hearer is a bit on the dim side. It may be that the message is a particularly complicated one and therefore needs to be spelt out bit by bit. It may be that the speaker is by nature habitually anxious to make himself completely clear. (? It might be that certain occupations predispose people to use more than the usual number of tone-groups per clause? ? Teachers and broadcasters, for instance, who are used to having to make themselves completely clear, might tend to use marked distribution of tone-groups and information units more frequently than some other people?)

In general then what the distribution of tone-groups does is to vary the value as information of the different parts of a message. A given part of a message can be a whole information unit, a whole point to be noted, or only part of an information unit, part of a point to be noted, according to whether it is allocated a whole tone-group to itself or only part of a tone-group.

Sometimes the location of tone-group boundaries can make more precise distinctions in meaning.

The grammatical difference and the difference in meaning between the sentence

Ex. 7^1.4 ||| || *The houses* [[*which were of historic interest*]] | *were destroyed* | *by fire* || |||

and the sentence

Ex. 7^1.11 ||| $^{||}$ *The houses, ((which were of historic interest,)) were destroyed | by fire* $^{||}$ |||

were discussed in Chapter 7, Section 4.2 of Volume 1, as were also the grammatical difference and the difference in meaning between the sentence

Ex. 7^1.12 ||| $^{||}$ *My wife* ⟦ *who lives in Rio de Janeiro* ⟧ *| sent | me | a Christmas card* $^{||}$ |||

and the sentence

Ex. 7^1.13 ||| $^{||}$ *My wife, ((who lives in Rio de Janeiro)), sent | me | a Christmas card* $^{||}$ |||....

It was pointed out in Chapter 7 of Volume 1 that the grammatical and meaning differences between the sentences would be reflected in spoken English by the phonological differences between the sentences. The main phonological difference between the sentences is the location of tone-group boundaries. The first sentence of each pair has two tone-groups, the boundary between them coming immediately after the rank-shifted clause:

Ex. 7^1.4   // *The houses which were of historic interest // were destroyed by fire //*
Ex. 7^1.12   // *My wife who lives in Rio de Janeiro // sent me a Christmas card //*

The second sentence of each pair has three tone-groups, the boundaries coming immediately before and immediately after the dependent clause:

Ex. 7^1.11   // *The houses, // which were of historic interest, // were destroyed by fire //*
Ex. 7^1.13   // *My wife, // who lives in Rio de Janeiro, // sent me a Christmas card //*

In the first sentence of each pair the location of the tone-group boundary shows that the rank-shifted clause is an integral part of the subject of the main clause. In the second sentence of each pair the location of a tone-group boundary on either side of the dependent clause shows that the dependent clause is separate from the main clause. This, then, is an example of a meaningful choice between different locations of tone-group boundaries.

A second set of choices relating to the tone-group is between a number of different **tones**; each tone-group chooses between a number of differently shaped intonation patterns.

The tones differ from each other in various ways. The parts of the tones carried by the tonic elements of tone-groups, as might be expected, differ more markedly than the parts of the tones carried by the pretonic elements. However the pretonic parts of the tones do differ to some extent.

There are three main ways in which the tones differ from each other. They differ in direction of pitch movement, in height of pitch and in range of pitch.

The direction of pitch movement of a tone may be **falling**, **rising**, **level**, or a combination of any two of these, or all three. In the conversation

Ex. 4.42 A. *I'm going to London for a weekend in March and I'm wondering where to stay*

B. *(to wife) Where's that place that I usually stay when I go to London?*

B's wife. *You stay at The Piccadilly.*

A. *You stay at The Piccadilly?*

B. *Yes, and if you want my advice, you stay at The Piccadilly!*

the first occurrence of the stretch of language *You stay at The Piccadilly* would in all probability be a tone-group which had chosen a tone with a predominantly falling pitch movement.

Ex. 4.43 // Λ *You* / *stay at The* / *Picca* / *dilly* //

(pretonic)　　　　　　　(tonic)

The pre-tonic would be level, while the tonic would consist of a steep fall followed by a less steep fall. The tonic would begin at about the same pitch as the pretonic ended. The second occurrence of the stretch of language *You stay at The Piccadilly* would probably be a tone-group which had chosen a tone with a predominantly rising pitch movement.

Ex. 4.44 // Λ *You* / *stay at The* / *Picca* / *dilly* //

(pretonic)　　　　　　　(tonic)

The pretonic would again probably be level, while the tonic would consist of a steep rise followed by a less steep rise. There would probably be a drop in pitch between the end of the pretonic and the beginning of the tonic. It is the difference in the direction of the pitch movement of the two occurrences of this stretch of language which shows that the first occurrence is a statement, while the second is a question.

Height of pitch varies from **low**, through **mid-low, mid** and **mid-high**, to **high**. A further difference between the tones chosen by the two occurrences of *You stay at The Piccadilly* discussed above is the difference in the height of their pitch. The tone chosen by the first occurrence would probably have a mid pretonic followed by a tonic falling from mid to low. The tone chosen by the second occurrence would probably have a high pretonic followed by a tonic rising from mid-low to high. Thus the first tone, both at its lowest point and at its highest point, is lower than the second tone.

Range of pitch varies from **narrow** through **medium** to **wide**. The second tone discussed above has a pitch range which is on the widish side of medium, since the pitch ranges from mid-low to high. As was said above this is probably the tone which would be used for the second occurrence of *You stay at The Piccadilly,* in which case it would be expressive of mild interest or mild surprise. It would however be possible to use for this occurrence a tone with an even wider pitch range, with the tonic rising from low to high, instead of from mid-low to high. This tone would be expressive of more than mild surprise, perhaps even of incredulity. It would be the range of pitch which would indicate the degree of surprise.

The third set of choices relating to the tone-group is the set which is concerned with where in the tone-group to put the tonic element.

As was said in Section 4.1 the tonic is usually placed at the end of its tone-group. The tonic element is usually the last foot in the tone-group. The most usual way of saying examples

Ex. 4.20 // Λ *I've* / *put the* / *book on the* / ***table*** //
Ex. 4.45 // *What shall I* / ***ask for?*** //

would be to place the tonic on *table* and *ask for* respectively, as indicated by the bold type. However, as was pointed out in Section 4.1, it would be possible to say

Ex. 4.21 // Λ *I've* / *put the* / ***book on the*** / *table* //

with the tonic element on *book on the* instead of on the last foot. Similarly it would be possible to say

Ex. 4.46 // *What shall* / ***I*** / *ask for?* //

with the tonic element on *I* instead of on the last foot. There is a choice, then, between a usual or unmarked position for the tonic and an unusual or marked position for the tonic. If the marked position is chosen, attention is drawn to the **new** bit of information contained in the utterance. The speaker of 4.21 is really saying 'You know I've put something on the table. Well, the something that I've put on the table is the book.' Everything except the book is already known to the speaker's audience. The book is the new bit of information. Similarly, the speaker of Ex. 4.46 is really saying 'I know what you're going to ask for. What I want to know is what I'm going to ask for.' The new bit of information is␣I.

There are three main sets of choices relating to the foot.

One set of choices relates to the location of foot boundaries.

As was pointed out in Section 4.1, it is possible to say either

Ex. 4.11 *// Come and / see me in my / office to- / morrow //* or
Ex. 4.15 *// Come and see / me in my / office to- / morrow //.*

The difference between these two utterances lies partly in the tonicity (the tonic element of Ex. 4.11 is *office to-*, while the tonic element of Ex. 4.15 is *me in my*), partly in the location of one of the foot boundaries. In Ex. 4.11 the initial boundary of the second foot occurs before *see*; in example Ex. 4.15 it occurs before *me*. In Ex. 4.11 *see* is carrying the stressed or salient element of the foot; in Ex. 4.15 the salient element is carried by *me*. Ex. 4.11 has the foot boundary in an unmarked position. It is perfectly usual for a verb to carry stress. One scarcely notices the stress since it is what one expects. The stress on *me* in Ex. 4.15 is much more noticeable since it is rather less usual for a pronoun to carry stress. Ex. 4.15 has the foot boundary in a marked position.

A second choice is the choice between sound and silence. A foot can choose between being sounded, partially silent, or silent.

A silent or partially silent foot acts in the same way as a punctuation mark, such as a comma or a full-stop, does in written English. It separates off units of information from each other. The silent foot in

Ex. 4.19 *// What are you / reading? // Λ / Shakespeare? //*

makes it clear that the utterance contains two separate questions. A partially silent foot is perhaps more analogous to a comma, while a silent foot is more analogous to a full-stop or question mark, though there is no exact correspondence between the phonological items and their graphological counterparts.

The third set of choices relating to the foot are the choices of pace. A foot can choose between being hurried, neutral or leisured.

The English Language is a stress-timed language. This means that the stressed syllables occur at roughly regular intervals of time. About the same amount of time elapses between the beginning of the salient element of the first foot in a tone-group and the beginning of the salient element of the second foot, as elapses between the beginning of the salient element of the second foot and the beginning of the salient element of the third foot. Each foot in a tone-group takes a roughly equal amount of time. This is true regardless of how many syllables there are in a foot. A foot with five syllables takes roughly the same amount of time to say as a foot with one syllable. In the utterance

Ex. 4.10 // *Thank you for* / *giving me such a* / *wonderful* / *time* //

the foot *giving me such a* takes roughly the same amount of time to say as the foot *time.*

Since the five syllables of a five-syllabled foot have to share the same amount of time as the syllable of a monosyllabic foot gets all to itself, the five syllables each have only a small amount of time. A five-syllabled foot therefore sounds hurried. A monosyllabic foot on the other hand sounds leisurely, since all the time is spent on one syllable. A two or three-syllabled foot is usually not very noticeable either way and can be described as neutral.

(The English Language can here be contrasted with the French Language. French is a syllable-timed language. In French the syllables occur at regular intervals of time. Each syllable takes about the same amount of time to say. There is no variety in the amount of time spent on individual syllables, as there is in English.

However there is variety in French in the amount of time spent on individual feet. In this respect there is variety in French, but not in English. French is not a stress-timed language. The stresses do not occur at regular intervals, so the feet are not the same length.

A language cannot be both a stress-timed language and a syllable-timed language. If a language has feet of equal length, it cannot also have syllables of equal length, since feet consist of unequal numbers of syllables. A foot with five syllables must either take longer than a foot with one syllable or spend less time on each syllable than a foot with one syllable. A foot with five syllables cannot both take the same amount of time as a foot with one syllable and also spend the same time on each of its five syllables as the monosyllabic foot spends on its one syllable.)

In English, leisured feet are used in two main ways. They are used to bring something to a firm conclusion. This is particularly true of verse.* A leisured foot is frequently found at the end of a line of verse, marking the end of the line as the end. In the nursery-rhyme

*Abercrombie, 1964

Ex. 4.47 /Humpty- / Dumpty / sat on a / wall,
/Humpty- / Dumpty / had a great / fall,
/All the King's / horses and / all the King's / men,
/Couldn't put / Humpty to / gether a / gain. /

each of the lines ends with a monosyllabic foot. It is very largely the presence of a leisured foot that makes one realise one has reached the end of a line.

The second main way that leisured feet are used in English is to draw attention to something important which follows the leisured foot. A leisured foot often seems rather long-drawn out and this has the effect of keeping the reader or hearer in suspense for something. When the something eventually arrives it has the more impact as a result. This use of leisured feet is again common in verse. It is also found in counting. When one counts, one usually makes the *-nine* (of *twenty-nine, thirty-nine*, etc.) a leisured foot. The beginning of each new set of ten (*thirty, forty*, etc.) has greater impact through following a leisured foot.

Ex. 4.48 ... *twenty- / seven twenty- / eight twenty- / nine / thirty ...*
... *thirty- / seven thirty- / eight thirty- / nine / forty ...*
... *forty- / seven forty- / eight forty- / nine / fifty ...*

Interesting examples of the use of leisured feet in verse can be found in the poetry of Gerard Manley Hopkins. For instance in

Ex. 4.49 ... / sheer / plod makes / plough down / sillion ...
(The Windhover)

the leisured quality of the foot *sheer* makes the following *plod* seem all the more plodding.

There are two main sets of choices relating to the syllable. A syllable can choose between being **strong** (that is, stressed) and **weak** (that is, unstressed). It can also choose between being **long** (taking a comparatively large amount of time) and being **short** (taking a comparatively little amount of time). These choices are not meaningful in themselves, but they do enable syllables to combine to form feet and they do enable the resulting feet to make the contrasts which are made by feet.

There are two main sets of choices relating to the phoneme.

Firstly a phoneme can choose between being **vocalic** and being **consonantal**. This choice is rather like the syllable choices; it is not meaningful in itself but it does enable phonemes to combine to form syllables.

The second kind of choice is a more meaningful kind of choice. This is the choice of which particular individual phonemes to use.

If the phoneme *p* is chosen to combine with the phonemes *u* and *n*, the lexical item *pun* results. If on the other hand the phoneme *b* is chosen, the lexical item *bun* results. If the phoneme *d* is chosen, the lexical item *dun* results and if the phoneme *g* is chosen, the lexical item *gun* results. Each different choice of phoneme produces a different lexical item and thus signals a different meaning.

We have seen then that at the level of phonology there are a number of formal contrasts, and that most of these formal contrasts relate in some way to meaning contrasts. It is now time to consider how some of the meaning contrasts can be codified in systems.

We shall also consider how far the formal contrasts of phonology relate directly to meaning contrasts, how far they are relateable only indirectly via grammar and lexis. In general we can say that the higher on the phonological rank scale the formal contrasts we are concerned with, the more likely they are to be directly relateable to meaning contrasts.

We saw earlier in this section that contrasts between different distributions of tone-groups enabled a speaker to make contrasts between different information values for the various parts of a message. The speaker of a clause can choose to mean either 'I, the speaker, want you, the hearer, to take this message as a whole as a point to be noted' (e.g. Ex. 4.38) or 'I, the speaker, want you, the hearer, to extract two (or more) points from this message' (e.g. Ex. 4.39 and 40). If we summarise the meaning 'I, the speaker, want you, the hearer, to take this message as a whole as a point to be noted' by the term **simple information distribution** and if we summarise the meaning 'I, the speaker, want you, the hearer, to extract two (or more) points from this message' by the term **compound information distribution**, this then gives us the system:

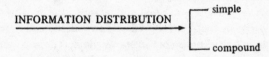

From this system Ex. 4.38 has chosen simple, while Ex. 4.39 and Ex. 4.40 have chosen compound. The terms of this system are realised directly by phonology, by the number of tone-groups allocated to the clause.

We also saw earlier in this section that contrasts between different positions of the tonic element within the tone-group enabled a speaker to focus attention on the newest bit of a particular message. A speaker can choose between meaning 'All of this message that I'm giving you is probably about equally new to you, though maybe the last bit of it is just a little bit newer than the rest' (e.g. Ex. 4.20) and meaning 'Most of this message that I'm giving you is very definitely known to you (or guessable by you) already. There is just one little bit of it which is new to you and I want you to focus your attention on that' (e.g. Ex. 4.21). If we summarise the meaning 'All of this message that I'm giving you is probably about equally new to you, though maybe the last bit of it is just a little bit newer than the rest' by the term **unmarked information focus** and if we summarise the meaning 'Most of this message that I'm giving you is very definitely known to you (or guessable by you) already. There is just one little bit of it which is new to you and I want you to focus your attention on that' by the term **marked information focus**, this then gives us the system.

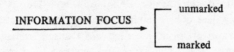

INFORMATION FOCUS ─────▶ ┌─ unmarked
                         └─ marked

From this system Ex. 4.20 and Ex. 4.45 have chosen unmarked, while Ex. 4.21 and Ex. 4.46 have chosen marked. The terms of the information focus system, like the terms of the information distribution system, are realised directly by phonology, the term unmarked information focus being realised by the placing of the tonic element in its most usual position at the end of a tone-group, the term marked information focus being realised by the placing of the tonic element in a less usual position somewhere other than at the end of a tone-group.

The other kind of contrast carried by the tone-group, the contrasts between different tones, enables a speaker, as we noted, to distinguish between such meanings as 'statement' and 'question' and between such meanings as 'mild surprise' and 'incredulity'. There is no room here to explore these meanings in detail, but it should be pointed out that they too form systems whose terms are realised directly by phonology.

At the other end of the scale we saw that the contrasts between particular individual phonemes enabled a speaker to distinguish between different formal items, the different formal items in turn distinguishing between different meanings. Here we have a case of phonological contrasts merely carrying a stage further the realisation of terms from grammatical and lexical systems. Terms from grammatical and lexical systems are realised by formal items, as we saw in Chapters 2 and 3. These formal items are in turn realised by combinations of phonological items, the particular individual phonemes.

4.4 DELICACY

Phonological systems can be related to each other on a scale of delicacy just as can grammatical systems. For instance, as we indicated in Section 4.3, by choosing a certain tone it is possible to express surprise and by choosing a particular variety of that tone it is possible to express a particular degree of surprise — mild surprise or great surprise. The choice of surprise is a less delicate choice than the choice of a particular degree of surprise. The second choice is dependent on the first.

When a particular language, or a particular variety of language, is being described, it is necessary for the phonological scale of delicacy to be interwoven with the grammatical scale of delicacy. This is because certain phonological choices are dependent on certain grammatical choices and vice versa. Certain areas of meaning are realised partially by grammar, partially by phonology. Questions, for instance, are realised in English by both grammar and phonology. The section of the scale of delicacy dependent on the term interrogative of the mood system includes both phonological systems and grammatical systems. Similarly the information distribution and information focus systems have a great deal in common with the theme systems of grammar and are usually included in the same network as the theme systems.

Perhaps a more realistic way of looking at it would be to say that there is really just one scale of delicacy for all meaning systems. It so happens that some of the systems on this scale specify moves on the grammatical and lexical sections of the scale of realisation, while others specify moves on the phonological section of the realisation scale.

4.5 REALISATION

We have seen that phonology realises terms from systems either directly, or indirectly via grammar and lexis. We have seen, that is, that terms from some systems directly specify certain phonological patterns, while terms from other systems specify moves on the grammatical and lexical sections of the realisation scale these moves leading eventually to formal items which in turn specify certain combinations of phonological items.

Phonology itself is realised by phonic substance. More exemplification of this is perhaps necessary than has so far been given.

Each particular phoneme can be realised by a number of different sounds; that is, by a number of different bits of phonic substance.

The phoneme *p,* for instance, occurs both in the word *penny* and in the word *tuppence.* The sound which realises the phoneme *p* in *penny* is a different sound from the sound which realises the phoneme *p* in *tuppence.* The *p* in *penny* is an aspirated *p,* while the *p* in *tuppence* is an unaspirated *p.* (*aspirated* means 'pronounced with an audible breath'.) The truth of this statement can be tested by putting a hand in front of the mouth, about three inches away from the mouth, and saying the words *penny* and *tup-pence* in turn. A greater amount of breath will be felt by the hand when *penny* is pronounced than when the word *tuppence* is pronounced.

Similarly, the words *cool, calm* and *collected* all begin with the same phoneme, but with different bits of phonic substance. The one phoneme is realised in three different ways in these three words. The tongue takes up a different position in the mouth for the pronounciation of the first sound of *cool* from the position it takes up for the pronounciation of the first sound of *calm,* and a different position yet again for the pronounciation of the first sound of *collected.*

The discussion of this chapter is combined with that of Chapter 5.

5
Graphology

Where all the other levels are concerned — context, grammar, lexis and phonology — the basic relationships between the levels are the same for all languages, though languages differ in matters of detail. However, the basic relationships between graphology and the other levels vary from language to language.

Languages can be grouped into two classes on the basis of the relationships between their graphology and their other levels. In one class of languages the graphological items, the symbols of writing, represent the formal items of a language. In the second class of languages, the graphological items represent the phonological items of a language. In a language of the first class there is a direct relationship between graphology and form, but no relationship between graphology and phonology; graphology and phonology are each independently related to form. In a language of the second class there is a direct relationship between graphology and phonology, but only an indirect relationship between graphology and form; graphology is related to form only via phonology. A language of the first class is said to have a **morphological script**. A language of the second class is said to have a **phonological script**.

Chinese script is an example of a morphological script. It is in fact the only example of a fully morphological script, though Japanese and Korean both have scripts which are partially morphological. In Chinese each written symbol represents a lexical item or a grammatical item. Each lexical item or grammatical item can also be represented by a sequence of sounds. There is no connection between the written symbol which represents a formal item and the sequence of sounds which represents the same formal item.

English is an example of a language with a phonological script. In English each written symbol represents a sound, and it is a combination of different sounds which represents a formal item. The letter *p,* for instance, does not on its own represent any formal item. What it represents is a phoneme, and this phoneme can combine with other phonemes to represent a lexical item, as in *pin.* There is, then, a direct relationship between symbol and sound in English. There is no direct relationship between symbol and formal item, but there is an indirect relationship between symbol and formal item via sound.

The statement that there is no direct relationship between symbol and formal item in English needs to be qualified. Most literate Englishmen, when encoding or decoding the written form of their language, move direct from form to graphology or vice versa without going via phonology. This is borne out by the fact that it is perfectly possible to write or read a word which one does not know how to pronounce. It is also borne out by the fact that there are what are sometimes called *spelling pronunciations*; that is pronunciations which have been influenced by spelling. The town of Wiveliscombe in Somerset was at one time usually pronounced 'Wilscombe' or 'Wulscombe' by the local inhabitants. These pronunciations are now going out of use in favour of a pronunciation which more nearly reflects the spelling of the name. It is evidently felt that it is the combination of letters – W, i, v, e, l, i, s, c, o, m, b, e, – which really represents the lexical item and that the sounds should represent the letters. The letters are thought to be primary and the sounds secondary, instead of the other way round. Even local inhabitants of long-standing now consider that they are being 'incorrect' when they say 'Wilscombe', since the sounds they use do not accurately represent the spelling. However, even if adult speakers of English do now by-pass phonology when reading or writing and even if they do show more respect for graphology than phonology, the fact remains that, when as children they learnt to read and write, there was no direct connection for them between symbol and formal item. The link between symbol and formal item was made for them by sound. They could not read or write until they were able to translate symbols into sounds. (This is true even of the 'Look and Say' method of teaching reading.) They would not now be able to make any connection between symbol and formal item if they had not at some time learnt the relation between symbol and sound. English graphology works through its relation with English phonology, even if in practice this does not always appear to be true.

5.1 UNITS

There is no general agreement among linguists as to what are the graphological units of English. One possible list is:
paragraph, orthographic sentence, sub-sentence, phrase, orthographic word, letter.

The term **paragraph** is used here in its usual sense. A paragraph is a stretch of language between two indentations.

The term **sentence** is also used in its usual sense. An orthographic sentence is a stretch of language between two full-stops. (The term *full-stops* here includes question-marks and exclamation-marks as well as full-stops proper.)

A **sub-sentence** is a stretch of language between two semi-colons, or between a full-stop and a semi-colon.

The term **phrase** is not used here in its usual sense. A phrase is a stretch of language between two commas, or between a comma and a full-stop, or between a comma and a semi-colon.

The term **word** is used in its usual sense. An orthographic word is a stretch of language between two spaces.

The term **letter** is also used in its usual sense. A letter is a single alphabetical symbol.

Like the units of other levels, the graphological units can be arranged on a rank scale. The rank scale for the English units listed above would be:

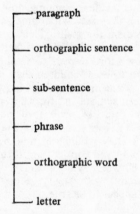

- paragraph
- orthographic sentence
- sub-sentence
- phrase
- orthographic word
- letter

However, as in the case of phonology, there is no possibility of rankshift for the graphological units. (Unless one regards quotation as graphological rankshift.)

Graphological units do not have structures in the way that the units of other levels do. Grammatical units carry patterns which can be described in grammatical terms. Lexical units carry patterns which can be described in lexical terms. Phonological units carry patterns which can be described in phonological terms.

Graphological units do not carry patterns which can be described in graphological terms. Graphological units do carry patterns, but the patterns which they carry are phonological or grammatical patterns, not graphological patterns.

For example the written version of each of the utterances

Ex. 7^1.11 || // *The houses, ((// which were of historic interest, //))*
         were destroyed by fire. // ||
Ex. 7^1.13 || // *My wife, ((// who lives in Rio de Janeiro, //)) sent me*
         a Christmas card. // ||

has three phrases. The first phrase of each utterance is bounded by a capital letter (implying a full-stop) and a comma, the second phrase by two commas, and the third phrase by a comma and a full-stop.

Although the boundaries of the phrases are graphologically marked, the phrases do not carry patterns which can be described in graphological terms. The patterns which the phrases of these utterances are carrying are phonological patterns. The phrases of the written versions of these utterances coincide with the tone-groups of the spoken versions. The phrases of the written versions are representing the tone-groups of the spoken versions. The phrases are providing information about what the written versions would sound like if spoken, about where the intonation patterns begin and end. The patterns which the phrases are carrying are the phonological patterns of the tone-groups they are representing.

The written version of each of the utterances

Ex. 7^1.4 || // *The houses* ⟦ *which were of historic interest* ⟧ // *were*
         destroyed by fire. // ||
Ex. 7^1.12 || // *My wife* ⟦ *who lives in Rio de Janeiro* ⟧ // *sent me a*
         Christmas card. // ||

has an orthographic sentence which consists of one sub-sentence which consists of one phrase.

In each case the phrase carries no patterns which can be described in graphological terms. The pattern which the phrase is carrying is here a grammatical pattern. In each utterance the phrase boundaries coincide with the clause boundaries. The phrase is representing the clause. It is showing where the clause begins and ends. The only pattern which the phrase is carrying is the SPCA structure of the clause. The phrase, like the clause it represents, forms the whole of the unit next above; the sub-sentence consists of only the one phrase and the clause-complex (grammatical sentence) consists of only one clause. The pattern which the sub-sentence is carrying is the α structure of the clause-complex. The patterns

which the graphological units are carrying are the grammatical patterns of
the grammatical units they represent.

There is an alternative way of punctuating Ex. 7^1.4 and Ex. 7^1.
'12:

.

Ex. 7^1.4a   ‖ // *The houses* ⟦ *which were of historic interest* ⟧ , // *were*
              destroyed by fire. // ‖
Ex. 7^1.12a   ‖ // *My wife* ⟦ *who lives in Rio de Janeiro* ⟧ , // *sent me a*
              Christmas card. // ‖

Each utterance now has two phrases.

These phrases are carrying phonological patterns as in Ex. 7^1.11 and
Ex. 7^1.13, not grammatical patterns as in Ex. 7^1.4 and Ex. 7^1.12. Their
boundaries coincide with the boundaries of tone-groups, not with the
boundaries of clauses. The phrases are representing tone-groups, not
clauses.

Examples 7^1.4 and 7^1.12 have the same meanings as Ex. 7^1.4a and
Ex. 7^1.12a. Examples 7^1.11 and 7^1.13 have different meanings from
Ex. 7^1.4 and 7^1.4a and Ex. 7^1.12 and 7^1.12a (see Chapter 7 of Volume
1). Both the kind of punctuation used in Ex. 7^1.4 and Ex. 7^1.12 and
the kind of punctuation used in Ex. 7^1.4a and Ex. 7^1.12a differentiate
their examples from Ex. 7^1.11 and Ex. 7^1.13. But the two kinds of
punctuation make the distinction by different methods.

The kind of punctuation used in Ex. 7^1.4 and Ex. 7^1.12 makes the
graphological unit, the phrase, coincide with the grammatical unit, the
clause, and the graphological unit, the sub-sentence, coincide with the
grammatical unit, the clause-complex. The fact that in each of these
examples the phrase forms the whole of the sub-sentence shows us that
the clause forms the whole of the clause-complex. In each of examples
Ex. 7^1.4 and Ex. 7^1.12 the clause-complex consists of one integrated
clause, which is not true of Ex. 7^1.11 and Ex. 7^1.13. The punctuation
in Ex. 7^1.4 and Ex. 7^1.12 makes the graphological units directly represent
the grammatical units in such a way that Ex. 7^1.4 and Ex. 7^1.12 are
shown to be different from Ex. 7^1.11 and Ex. 7^1.13.

The punctuation in Ex. 7^1.4a and Ex. 7^1.12a makes the graphological unit, the phrase, represent the phonological unit, the tone-group.
Examples 7^1.4a and 7^1.12a are shown to be different from Ex. 7^1.11
and Ex. 7^1.13 since each of Ex. 7^1.4a and Ex. 7^1.12a have two phrases
and therefore two tone-groups, while each of Ex. 7^1.11 and Ex. 7^1.13
have three phrases and therefore three tone-groups. This second kind of
punctuation shows the distinction by making graphological units rep-

resent phonological units, instead of by making graphological units represent grammatical units like the first kind of punctuation.

Although the second kind of punctuation does not make graphological units directly represent grammatical units, it does enable the graphological units to indirectly provide clues to the grammar. As we have seen in this chapter, the graphological units are, by the second kind of punctuation, made to represent phonological units. The location of the boundaries of phonological units can in turn provide clues to grammatical structure. The graphological units are able to provide clues to grammatical structure indirectly via the phonological units they represent.

There are, then, two possible ways of punctuating English. There is grammatical punctuation, making graphological units directly represent grammatical units, and there is phonological punctuation, making graphological units provide clues to grammar (and meaning) indirectly by making the graphological units represent phonological units.

Some writers of English use grammatical punctuation, some use phonological punctuation. Most writers use a mixture of the two, often in a rather haphazard and inconsistent fashion.

In the view of the present writer, phonological punctuation is more likely to help the reader than grammatical punctuation, though this cannot be taken to be an inviolable rule. However, unfortunately, grammatical punctuation is often considered to be more 'correct' than phonological punctuation.

Although graphological units carry the patterns of other levels, rather than their own patterns, graphological units do not regularly correspond with the units of any other level.

For instance, as has been shown in this chapter, phrase boundaries sometimes coincide with the tone-group boundaries of phonology and sometimes coincide with the clause boundaries of grammar. But phrases do not regularly correspond either with tone-groups or with clauses.

Similarly letters often correspond with phonemes, but not always. The letter *p* regularly represents the sound *p* (except when it is combined with another letter such as *h* or *n,* making a compound symbol, as in *phone* or *pneumonia*) and the letter *b* regularly represents the sound *b.* The letter *c,* however, can represent either the sound at the beginning of *cat* or the sound at the beginning of *ceiling.*

(For this reason it is not really correct to use ordinary alphabetical symbols when discussing sounds, as has so far been done in this book. It is all very well to write about the sound *p* and to use the letter *p* to stand for the sound, since these two do regularly correspond. But for other sounds, such as those represented by the letter *c,* it is necessary to use a special phonetic alphabet in order to make clear exactly which of the possible sounds is being discussed. The initial sound of *cat* is usually represented in the phonetic alphabet as [k], while the initial sound of *ceiling* is usually represented as [s].

Phonetic transcriptions are usually enclosed in square brackets.

Although very little has been said in this book about phonetics it should be stressed that a knowledge of phonetics is very important for the study of linguistics.)

5.2 CONTRASTS

The formal contrasts of graphology, the contrasts between symbols such as *?, !* and . and the contrasts between symbols such as *p, b, t* and *d*, realise meaning contrasts. But the realisation is always indirect: in the case of symbols such as *?, !* and ., the realisation is via phonology or grammar or both; in the case of symbols such as *p, b, t* and *d* the realisation is via phonology and lexis (or in the case of a language with a morphological script, via lexis alone).

For example, as has been shown, it is possible for the graphological unit, the phrase, to represent the phonological unit, the tone-group. By doing so it can indirectly carry the choices which relate to the location of tone-group boundaries. Different distributions of phrases can thus, indirectly, via phonology, realise the meaning distinctions which were shown in Chapter 4 to be realised by different distributions of tone-groups.

Graphology can provide some clues to the choices of tone made by the tone-group, and can thus, indirectly, via phonology, realise some of the meaning distinctions realised by the different tones. The question-mark at the end of the written version of

Ex. 4.44   *You stay at The Piccadilly?*

indicates that the spoken version of the utterance would have a rising intonation pattern and would therefore be a question.

However, graphology's ability to provide clues to tonal choices is very limited indeed. Graphology cannot indicate height of pitch or range of pitch, and in most utterances it does not accurately represent direction of pitch movement. It is true that graphology can be taken to be indicating direction of pitch movement in Ex. 4.44. The question-mark of this example does indicate rising intonation. But a question-mark by no means always indicates rising intonation. The question

Ex. 5.1   *Where are you going?*

for instance, would be more likely to be spoken with a falling intonation pattern. The questionness of this question is realised by the presence of the lexical item *Where* and by the grammatical structure P(S), rather than by the phonology. The question-mark of the written version of this question is really superfluous.

The most formal kinds of written English have no graphological means of indicating tonicity choices, the choices between different positions of the tonic element. Less formal kinds of written English, however, sometimes use underlining to indicate a marked positioning of the tonic. They are therefore, indirectly, able to distinguish between new information and known or guessable information.

So far the examples given of systems indirectly carried by graphological units have all been systems carried by the tone-group. The next example relates to systems carried by the unit at the other end of the phonological rank scale.

Letters, by representing phonemes, indirectly distinguish between lexical items and thus even more indirectly distinguish between the meanings carried by the lexical items. As shown in Chapter 4, the phonemes *p* and *b* distinguish the lexical item *pun* from the lexical item *bun.* By representing their respective phonemes, the letters *p* and *b* distinguish between these two lexical items in written English.

> Sometimes graphology distinguishes between lexical items which are not differentiated by phonology. *flower* and *flour*, for instance, are spelt differently though pronounced alike, as also are *tail* and *tale*, and *peer* and *pier.*
> Conversely, phonology sometimes distinguishes between lexical items which are not differentiated by graphology. *tear* meaning 'drop from eye' and *tear* meaning 'rent' for instance, are pronounced differently though spelt alike, as are also *bow* meaning 'knot of ribbon' and *bow* meaning 'obeisance', and *minute* meaning 'very small' and *minute* meaning 'sixtieth of an hour'.

We have seen that graphology can indirectly realise some of the systems which are really realised by phonology. Graphology cannot however realise some of the more delicate systems realised by phonology. The resources of graphology are much smaller than the resources of phonology. It is possible to vary the intonation of a stretch of language in a large number of ways, but it is only possible to vary the punctuation of a stretch of language in a small number of ways, if at all. Consequently, whereas phonology can make a large number of distinctions and very fine distinctions, graphology can make only a small number of distinctions and not very fine distinctions.

For instance, the more delicate of the two systems used in Chapter 4 to exemplify the phonological scale of delicacy would not be possible in graphology. It might be conceded that the question-mark at the end of Ex. 4.44 was indicative of surprise, but by no stretch of the imagination could the question-mark be thought to indicate the degree of surprise. Graphology can make certain fairly basic distinctions, but cannot make finer distinctions such as that between mild surprise and great surprise.

It is because the resources of graphology are so much smaller than those of phonology that more care over grammar and lexis needs to be taken when one is writing than when one is speaking. One cannot rely on graphology to resolve ambiguities in the way that phonology often disambiguates the grammar and lexis of spoken language.

5.3 REALISATION

In Chapter 2 graphology was placed in a position parallel to phonology on the scale of realisation. Readers will have gathered from this chapter that there is an alternative position for it.

If the encoding and decoding processes of language are considered in relation to an actual piece of writing by an adult user of a language, the position suggested for graphology in Chapter 2 is probably the most realistic one, since, as has been shown, when encoding or decoding, adults usually, or at any rate often, move direct from form to graphology or vice-versa.

However, if what is being considered is the more general question of how language works, it would be necessary to distinguish between a language such as Chinese and a language such as English. For Chinese the position suggested in Chapter 2 would be appropriate since Chinese graphology directly realises form. But for English it would be more realistic to place graphology to the right of phonology on the scale since there is a sense in which graphology can be said to realise phonology. Although there are sometimes direct links between graphology and form in English, English graphology in general can be said to function indirectly, via phonology, rather than directly.

5.4 DISCUSSION

5.4.1 *General Linguistics*

We have seen that language can be made manifest in two main ways: by means of spoken sounds, and by means of written symbols. We have seen that the spoken sounds of language represent the meanings of language, either directly, or indirectly via the forms of language. We have seen that the written symbols of language usually represent the forms and meanings of language indirectly via the spoken sounds, though we have noted that in a language such as Chinese the forms can be directly represented by the written symbols.

5.4.2 *Descriptive Linguistics*

It is perhaps self-evident that if a language or variety of a language is to be fully described its phonology and graphology must be described as well as its grammar and lexis. However graphological description sometimes tends to get neglected.

5.4.3 *Contrastive Linguistics*

We have noted that very basic differences can exist between languages in the ways in which their graphology relates to their phonology and their form.

In matters of phonological and graphological detail interesting contrasts can be found between different varieties of a language.

For instance, in these days of disappearing dialects, the greatest differences between the regional varieties of English lie in their phonology.

Registers too differ in their phonology. Abercrombie (1963) has drawn attention to some of the phonological differences between conversation and what he calls 'spoken prose'.

Written registers can differ in their graphology. For instance, underlinings, dashes, double or treble exclamation marks are accepted methods of punctuating in some registers but not in others. Some registers show a greater tendency towards phonological punctuation, while others show a preference for grammatical punctuation.

Another interesting line of inquiry is to contrast spoken registers with written registers in such a way as to see how far the differences between them are conditioned by the differing resources of phonology and graphology.

An understanding of the relationships between phonology and graphology is important for a historical study of a language. Since we have no tape-recordings dating from the Old and Middle English periods, we cannot study Old and Middle English phonology directly. We have to try to deduce it from the graphology.

5.4.4 *Applied Linguistics*

There are many applications of phonological and graphological studies. Just three will be mentioned here.

In the past, discussions of the prosody of English verse have been bedevilled by attempts to impose on English verse methods of scansion appropriate to Latin verse or French verse. What is needed is a new approach to English prosody which will take into account what is known about how English phonology works (as opposed to what is known about how French phonology works or what is thought about how Latin phonology worked). Abercrombie (1964) has provided the beginnings of such an approach.

An understanding of the relationships between the graphology of a language and the phonology of a language is very relevant to the initial teaching of children to read and write. The importance of such an understanding for this purpose is discussed by Mackay and Thompson (1968).

At a later stage in their education it is usually thought necessary to teach children something about punctuation. A discussion of how graphology relates to the other levels of language, of exactly what kind of information is encoded in punctuation (phonological information? grammatical information? semantic information? or a combination of these?), would surely be of greater value in giving them a real understanding of what they are doing when they punctuate than would an attempt merely to teach them a list of 'rules' in the traditional fashion.

5.4.5 *Systemic Linguistics and Other Schools of Linguistics*

It is perhaps true to say that over the years systemic linguists have paid more attention to graphology than have the linguists of some other schools.

6
Context

Context can be thought of as the level which is concerned with the meaning of language.

We have of course been considering meaning all the way through the book. We have many times, when focussing on the other levels, crossed the boundary into context. The study of meaning is fundamental to language study and it is impossible to adequately consider the other levels without taking meaning into account.

The purpose of this chapter is, as is fitting for a final chapter, to summarise and draw together threads which have been introduced earlier and to end the book by focussing attention on this most important of all aspects of linguistics, the study of meaning.

6.1 CONTEXTUAL MEANING AND FORMAL MEANING

Systemic linguistics distinguishes between two different kinds of meaning: **contextual meaning** and **formal meaning.** It is contextual meaning that we are primarily concerned with in this chapter, but it will perhaps be helpful if a certain amount of space is devoted also to formal meaning.

6.1.1 *Contextual Meaning*

Contextual meaning is what most people mean by the term *meaning* when they use it in everyday conversation. Contextual meaning is the relationship between a formal item or pattern and an element of situation; that is, between a formal item or pattern and something which is outside the language itself, something which belongs to the world around.

For instance, the English lexical item *man* has contextual meaning. Users of English regularly associate the item *man* with objects looking like this 大 which occur in the world around. The relationship between the item *man* and the objects 大 大 大 大 is the regular association made between them by users of English. The contextual meaning of the item *man* is the relationship of regular association which it has with the objects 大 大 大 大.

The same relationship of regular association applies between the item *leap* and certain actions which occur in the world. The same relationship applies between the item *clever* and certain qualities which are perceivable in the world. In each case there is a relationship of regular association between a linguistic item and something which is **extra-linguistic**, something which is part of the situation of language rather than part of the language itself.

The statement that contextual meaning is what most people mean by the term *meaning* in everyday conversation should perhaps be qualified. The term *contextual meaning* really has a wider meaning than that which most people give to the term *meaning*. As was explained in Chapter 1, situation can be subdivided into thesis, immediate situation and wider situation. What most people think of as meaning is the relationship between a formal item and an element of thesis. However there can also be a relationship of regular association between a formal item and an element of immediate situation, or a relationship of regular association between a formal item and an element of wider situation. Both these kinds of relationship are included in contextual meaning as well as the relationship between a formal item and an element of thesis.

The relationships discussed above between *man* and certain objects, between *leap* and certain actions, between *clever* and certain qualities, are all examples of relationships between formal items and elements of thesis. Examples of the second kind of contextual relationship, that between a formal item and an element of immediate situation, are provided by the items *grub* (= food) and *luncheon*. When the item *grub* is used, there are usually present in the immediate situation such elements as informality, familiarity between speaker and hearer, social equality between speaker and hearer. The item *grub* is regularly associated with informality, familiarity, social equality. It has a relationship of regular association with these elements of immediate situation. When the item *luncheon* (as opposed to *lunch*) is used, there are usually present in the immediate situation such elements as formality, ceremony, special occasion. The item *luncheon* is regularly associated with formality, ceremony, special occasion. It has a relationship of regular association with these elements of immediate situation.

Examples of the third kind of contextual relationship, that between a formal item and an element of wider situation, are provided by the items *with it, trendy, switched on* (all with the sense of 'up-to-date'); *afters, pudding, sweet, dessert* (all referring to the course which follows the main course of a meal); *mommet* (= scarecrow), *suant* (= smooth). When the items *with it, trendy, switched on,* are used, the wider situation of the user usually includes either the element of belonging to a particular generation or the element of having spent quite a lot of time with members of that generation. Each of the items *afters, pudding, sweet, dessert,* is associated with a particular kind of social or educational background on the part of its users. When the items *mommet* or *suant* are used, the wider situation of the user usually includes the element of having spent a good deal of time in Devonshire or the element of being related to someone who has spent a good deal of time in Devonshire. All these items have relationships of regular association with elements of the wider situation of their users.

Each of these three kinds of relationship between an item and situation enables the item, when it is used, to provide a certain kind of information.

When the item *fag* (= cigarette) is used, for instance, it communicates three different kinds of information, each of the three kinds of information being the result of one of the kinds of relationship between the item and situation.

On each occasion that it is used, the item *fag* provides the information that its user is thinking about an object which looks like this ⌇ . The process by which this information is conveyed can be diagrammed as follows:

The speaker   The hearer

The speaker thinks of an element of thesis (T), in this case the object ⌇, and utters an item (I), in this case the item *fag,* which he associates with the object. The hearer hears the item and thinks of the associated object. The speaker has successfully transferred his thought to his hearer. He is able to do so because he is able to make the link between the object and the item, and because his hearer is able to make the link between the item and the object. The reason that they are both able to make the necessary links is that both know of the relationship of regular association between the object and the item. There may or may not be an actual cigarette in the room at the time. If the speaker says 'Like a fag?' there is likely to be a cigarette present. If the speaker says 'Wish I had a fag!' there is likely to be no cigarette present. Both utterances successfully communicate the thought of the object ⌇. It does not matter whether or not the object is actually present. The speaker's and hearer's knowledge of the regular association between the item *fag* and the object ⌇ make the actual presence of a cigarette unnecessary. By using the item *fag* to represent the object, the speaker is able to make his hearer think of the object 🚬 just as successfully as if he had pointed to an actual cigarette. The relationship of regular association between a formal item and an element of thesis, then, enables a speaker to provide his hearer with information about what it is he is thinking about.

The item *fag* also has a relationship of regular association with elements of immediate situation. Like the item *grub* it is usually associated with informality, familiarity, social equality. When the item *fag* is used it indicates that the situation in which it is being used has these qualities. If the situation in which it is being used already contains clues to its informality, familiarity, social equality — facial expressions, gestures, other linguistic items associated with informality — then the information provided by the item *fag* about its immediate situation will be merely corroborative. However it is quite possible for the item *fag* to be used in an immediate situation in which there have not as yet been any indications of informality. In this case it will be providing new information. Because it is usually associated with informality it will at once introduce an element of informality into its immediate situation even if the situation has hitherto been formal. Sometimes a speaker will deliberately use in a rather formal situation an item like *fag* which is associated with informality. He usually does so in order to communicate to his hearers the information that he wishes the conversation to proceed on a more friendly and less formal basis than it has up to then. Sometimes a speaker will, for comic effect, use in one kind of situation an item which is usually associated with a different kind of situation. The discrepancy between the item's usual kind of immediate situation and the kind of immediate situation in which it is being used on that particular occasion will indicate the humorous tone of the speaker's remarks. In reported speech the items through their associations create or recreate their own immediate situations. If a man A is talking to a man B about what a man C said, B can gather from A's repetition of the items used by C some information about the situation in which C originally used the items. If A says 'And he said to me "Got a fag?" ', B will gather that the situation A is describing was an informal one. Novelists of course make a great deal of use of items with this kind of association in order to suggest the atmosphere of the situations they are describing. The relationship of regular association between a formal item and elements of immediate situation, then, enables a speaker or writer to provide information about the atmosphere or tone of a situation.

The item *fag* also seems to be acquiring a relationship of regular assocication with an element of wider situation. The item seems to be going out of use among the younger generation. It seems to be associated more with older age-groups. The use of the item now seems to date one; by using it one provides one's hearers with information about one's age. The relationship between a formal item and elements of wider situation enables the item to provide information about its user's background.

The item *fag*, then, has relationships of regular association with an element of thesis, with elements of immediate situation and with an element of wider situation. Through these relationships it is able, when it is used, to provide three different kinds of information: it refers to a particular kind of object; it indicates something about the social atmosphere of the occasion on which it is used; and it suggests something about its user's age. These three kinds of information are all part of what is communicated by the item. Together they make up the total information conveyed by the item.

The kind of information resulting from an item's relationship with an element of thesis and the kind resulting from an item's relationship with an element of immediate situation are perhaps more central to the information given by the item than is the kind of information resulting from the item's relationship with an element of wider situation. Certainly the first two kinds of information are more intentional on the part of the speaker than the third. A speaker usually does intend to communicate his thesis. He usually does, though perhaps rather less consciously as a general rule, intend to give the right sort of impression of his immediate situation. He usually does not, however, intend to communicate anything about his own background. Sometimes the reverse is true; sometimes a speaker feels distressed if he has 'given himself away' by his choice of linguistic items. The third kind of information is usually communicated in spite of the speaker's intentions rather than because of them.

All the examples of contextual relationships so far given in this chapter have been examples of relationships between lexical items and elements of situation. Other levels of language also have contextual relationships with elements of situation. This is another way in which contextual meaning is wider than what most people mean by the term *meaning*. Most people think of meaning as belonging only to lexical items and combinations of lexical items. They do not realise that other levels of language also have meaning.

That the level of grammar has meaning can be demonstrated by a discussion of the first stanza of *Jabberwocky* from Lewis Carroll's *Through the Looking Glass*:

> 'Twas brillig, and the slithy toves
>   Did gyre and gimble in the wabe;
> All mimsy were the borogoves,
>   And the mome raths outgrabe.

Jabberwocky cannot really be said to have lexical contextual meaning. Most of the lexical items in the poem have no relationship of regular association with any elements of situation. At the point in the book at which the poem first appears they have no kind of association, regular or otherwise, though later in the book Humpty Dumpty does provide some sort of association for some of them. Yet the poem does have some meaning even at the point at which it first appears. Alice herself says of it, *'Somehow it seems to fill my head with ideas – only I don't exactly know what they are!'* It is for the most part the grammar of the poem which provides what meaning it does have, which fills Alice's head with ideas.

The last clause of the first stanza, *And the mome raths outgrabe,* has a structure which includes a predicator. The clause has chosen the term major. From this Alice could have gathered the information that some sort of process was going on. The clause has no complement. It cannot therefore have chosen the term relational process (since relational process clauses have complements) and must have chosen the term material process or the term mental process. Alice could not only have deduced that there was a process going on; she could have deduced something about the kind of process that was going on. She could in fact have gone further. The absence of a complement also makes it likely that the clause has chosen restricted process and middle. (There are other possibilities here, such as non-middle and intransitive, but we usually interpret something in the most likely way unless we are given positive information to the contrary.) So it would appear that the process was the kind of process which involves only one set of participants, that set of participants being in the role of performer of the process. Thus Alice could not only have made deductions about the process itself; she could also have made deductions about the participants in the process, about the number of sets of participants involved and the roles they were playing. Furthermore the presence of an *s* ending in the subject group and the absence of an *s* ending from the predicator group show that the term plural has been chosen. Although there is only one set of participants involved in the action, this set consists of more than one person or thing; there was more than one performer of the process. From the grammar of this clause, then, Alice could have learnt quite a lot about the process and the participants of the situation which the clause describes. To misquote Alice herself 'Some people or things did something: that's clear, at any rate.'

The second clause of the stanza, *and the slithy toves Did gyre and gimble in the wabe,* has a similar structure to that of the last clause. It therefore provides similar information about the situation it is describing. It also provides additional information. The structure of the second clause includes an adjunct. This indicates that there was some special circumstance in which the process was taking place. The predicator group has two v elements. This indicates that there were two processes going on in the situation being described.

The third clause of the stanza, *All mimsy were the borogoves,* is describing a rather different kind of situation. This clause is like the other two in that its structure includes a predicator, which indicates that there is a process involved in its situation, but there the resemblance ends. This clause has a complement and the complement is the kind of complement which is usually associated with a relational process clause. (The headword of the complement group, *mimsy,* has a *y* ending which suggests that it is an adjective. Adjective headwords are characteristic of the complement groups of a certain kind of relational process clause.) The process of the third clause's situation is a qualitative process. No-one is doing anything, but someone or something possesses some quality or characteristic. The situation of this clause involves two sets of participants, a set of participants to which the quality is being ascribed, and a set which consists of the quality itself.

The first clause, *'Twas brillig,* is like the third clause and similar deductions can be made about the information it provides.

As we saw in Chapters 4 and 5, the levels of phonology and graphology usually have contextual meaning via grammar and lexis rather than directly. Phonology and graphology are meaningful in that they realise the items and patterns, and thus the terms from systems, of lexis and grammar.

However we did note in Chapter 4 that phonology did have some direct links with meaning. We saw, for instance, that meaning such as simple and compound information distribution and unmarked and marked information focus were directly realised by phonology.

It should perhaps be mentioned here that very occasionally there is also another kind of direct link between phonology and meaning, that there is another kind of regular association between something phonological and something extra-linguistic, something situational. For instance items such as *bang, crackle, miaou, tu-whit-tu-whoo, splash, tinkle* do to a certain extent reproduce in their own sound the sound of the element of situation which they represent. Items such as *flutter, flicker, flitter,* though not actually reproducing any sound, nevertheless suggest through their own sound some characteristic of the actions they represent. Similarly items such as *slime, sludge, slurp* suggest through their sound some characteristic of the things they represent. We should not however get this out of proportion. Items such as these form only a very small minority of the total vocabulary of English.

A direct link between graphology and situation is even rarer than a direct link between phonology and situation. A direct link between graphology and situation is usually found only in the works of literary writers who are deliberately using language in an unusual way.

One example of this is the back-to-front writing of *Jabberwocky* indicating that the poem comes from Looking-Glass Country.

Another example is George Herbert's poem *Easter Wings* in which the lines are arranged in such a way as to make each stanza look like a pair of wings.

A third example is E. E. Cummings' poem *anyone lived in a pretty how town.* This poem has only two full stops and only two capital letters. There is a full stop at the end of the first stanza followed by a capital letter at the beginning of the second stanza and there is a full stop at the end of the last-but-one stanza followed by a capital letter at the beginning of the last stanza. There is no capital letter at the beginning of the poem and no full stop at the end of the poem. The fact that the middle section of the poem, stanzas two to eight, is enclosed between a capital letter and a full stop suggests that it is dealing with something that has a beginning and an end. The fact that the poem does not begin with a capital and does not end with a full stop suggests that the poem as a whole is concerned with something that cannot be said to have a beginning and an end. Something finite has been set in the middle of something infinite. One of the main points that the poem is making, as we learn from the other levels of language, is that, whereas the life of any one man sooner or later comes to an end and is forgotten, life in general goes on unaffected by the life or death of an individual. Something finite, the life of an individual, is seen in relation to something infinite, life in general. Thus the graphology makes a direct contribution to one aspect of the meaning of the poem.

6.1.2 *Formal Meaning*

Contextual meaning, then, is the relationship between a linguistic item, pattern or term from a system and an element of situation. It is a relationship between things at different points on the scale of realisation.

Formal meaning on the other hand is the relationship between a linguistic item, pattern or term from a system and other linguistic items, patterns or terms from systems belonging to the same level of language. Formal meaning is a relationship between things at the same point on the scale of realisation.

The formal meaning of a lexical item is its potentiality for collocating with other lexical items and its potentiality for contrasting with other lexical items.

The formal meaning of the lexical item *cat,* for instance, is its ability to collocate with *mew, purr, lap, milk, fur, tail,* etc. and its ability to contrast with *dog, mouse, kitten,* etc. A complete statement of the formal meaning of the lexical item would involve a comprehensive list of all the other lexical items with which it could collocate and a comprehensive list of all the other lexical items with which it could contrast. A complete statement would also involve an assessment of the likelihood of the item collocating with or contrasting with each of the items on the lists.

The formal meaning of a grammatical item or pattern is its potentiality for collocating with other grammatical items and patterns, its potentiality for contrasting with other grammatical items and patterns, and its potentiality for being substituted for other grammatical items and patterns.

The formal meaning of the grammatical item *drank,* for instance, includes its ability to occur with *he, she, John, Mary, the horse,* etc. preceding it and its ability to occur with *water, beer, a pint,* etc. following it (but not with *water, beer, a pint,* etc. preceding it and not with *he, she, John, Mary, the horse,* etc. following it.) The formal meaning also includes the item's ability to contrast with *drink* and *drunk.* The formal meaning also includes the fact that *drank* is grammatically substitutable for *ate, sewed, chose, broke,* etc. (but not for *John, horse, beer,* etc. or for *happy, beautiful, nasty,* etc. or even for *was, became, seemed,* etc.)

It should not be forgotten of course that in grammar we are concerned with formal items as members of classes, not as individual items.

The formal meaning of a phonological or graphological item or pattern is its potentiality for occurring with other phonological or graphological items and patterns and its potentiality for contrasting with other phonological or graphological items and patterns.

The formal meaning of the phonological item *p,* for instance, is its ability to occur with *r, l,* etc. and its ability to contrast with *b, t, d,* etc.

The term *formal meaning* often worries people who meet it for the first time, since the use of the term *meaning* here is so far removed from the usual use of the term. The term *contextual meaning* presents much less difficulty, since although this use of the term *meaning* extends the everyday sense of the term it does not radically change it.

It would perhaps be helpful to think of formal meaning as 'the means of meaning' rather than actually as 'meaning'. Contextual meaning could then be regarded as 'meaning proper'. It is through its formal meaning that language is able to have contextual meaning. It is because of its formal contrasts and patterns that language is able to have regular associations with elements of situation. Before an item can become regularly associated with an element of situation it must be identifiable as a distinct item. An item takes its identity from the patterns in which it occurs and the contrasts into which it enters. Language itself is structured and it is therefore able to express in an ordered way generalisations about situation.

We are here making explicit what has been implicit all the way through the book. Level by level through the book we have been examining the formal patterns and contrasts of language, the formal meaning, and then considering the relationships between the formal items and patterns and elements of situation, the contextual meaning, showing how the one makes possible the other.

6.2   TYPES OF CONTEXTUAL MEANING

In Section 6.1.1 we saw that all levels of language have contextual meaning: that lexis and grammar always have contextual meaning; that phonology sometimes has contextual meaning; and that graphology very occasionally has contextual meaning.

We considered very informally in Section 6.1.1 some different types of contextual meaning (mainly in relation to lexis). We saw that sometimes regular associations are with elements of thesis, sometimes with elements of immediate situation, sometimes with elements of wider situation.

Let us now explore in greater detail these different types of contextual meaning. We shall have room in this section only to explore them in relation to grammar, but it should be stressed that both the contextual meaning of lexis and the contextual meaning of grammar (and indeed the contextual meaning of phonology and graphology, in so far as these levels have contextual meaning) can be subdivided in this way.

6.2.1   *Experiential Meaning*

The examples of grammatical contextual meaning given in Section 6.1.1, those from the first stanza of *Jabberwocky,* were all of the same type. They all provided information about the processes of a situation, the participants in these processes, and the relationships between them. They all in fact had to do with the thesis situation, the situation which was being described.

This type of contextual meaning is called **experiential** meaning.

6.2.2 *Logical Meaning*

There is more that we can learn from the grammar of the first stanza of *Jabberwocky*. The stanza consists of one sentence whose structure is $\alpha \, \alpha \, \alpha \, \alpha$. The first and second clauses are linked by *and,* as are also the third and fourth clauses. The second and third clauses are linked simply by being juxtaposed to each other on either side of a semi-colon. Each clause can be said to be describing a mini-situation which forms part of a maxi-situation described by the stanza as a whole (which in turn forms part of the even larger situation described by the poem as a whole). The grammar provides information about the way in which the mini-situations are related to each other in order to form the maxi-situation. The $\alpha \, \alpha \, \alpha \, \alpha$ structure of the sentence and the kind of link between the elements show that the mini-situations of the stanza simply co-exist in the maxi-situation. There is no stronger relationship between them. If Lewis Carroll had written

'Twas brillig, but the slithy toves
  Did gyre and gimble in the wabe;
Since mimsy were the borogoves,
  The mome raths outgrabe.

the use of *but* instead of *and* would have indicated a more definite relationship between the mini-situations of the first and second clauses, while the use of *since* instead of *and* together with the $\beta \, \alpha$ structure would have indicated a more definite relationship between the mini-situations of the third and fourth clauses. However Lewis Carroll is using an impressionistic technique whereby he is simply juxtaposing mini-situations in order to create a maxi-situation. The only relationship between his mini-situations to which he wishes to draw attention is that of co-existence.

This second kind of grammatical meaning — the kind which provides information about the way in which mini-situations are related within a maxi-situation — is called **logical meaning.**

Both experiential and logical meaning relate to the thesis part of situation. Both provide information about the situation or situations that the language is about, the situation or situations that the language is describing. Experiential and logical meaning are sometimes grouped together under the heading **ideational meaning**.

6.2.3 *Interpersonal Meaning*

Grammar can also provide information about immediate situation.

All the clauses in the first stanza of *Jabberwocky* have chosen the term declarative from the system of mood. This indicates that the immediate situation of the first stanza is one in which a speaker or writer wishes to inform a hearer or reader of something. It also indicates that the speaker or writer is not expecting any obvious response from his audience. (If the clauses had chosen the term interrogative, this would have indicated that the speaker or writer was expecting some kind of reply, in the form of words or gestures, from the hearer or reader. If the clauses had chosen the term imperative this would have indicated that the speaker or writer was expecting some kind of action in response to his remark.)

The third, fourth, fifth and seventh stanzas of the poem, like the first stanza, have clauses which have all chosen the term declarative (except for a couple of minor clauses which cannot choose from the system of mood). This indicates that they have a similar immediate situation to that of the first stanza. Like the first stanza they are spoken by the narrator in his own person. A narrator's main purpose can be said to be informational, the telling of a story rather than the eliciting of replies or actions from his audience.

The second stanza

> *'Beware the Jabberwock, my son!*
> *The jaws that bite, the claws that catch!*
> *Beware the Jubjub bird, and shun*
> *The frumious Bandersnatch!'*

and the sixth stanza

> *'And hast thou slain the Jabberwock?*
> *Come to my arms, my beamish boy!*
> *O frabjous day! Callooh! Callay!'*
> *He chortled in his joy.*

each include clauses which have chosen the term interrogative or the term imperative from the system of mood. The second stanza and the first three lines of the sixth stanza have a different immediate situation from that of the rest of the poem. The narrator is not here speaking in his own person and the audience of the poem is not here being directly addressed. A character in the actual story is speaking and is presumably addressing another character in the story. In the second stanza the first character's main purpose is to ensure that the second character takes certain action. In the sixth stanza the first character begins by asking a question, presumably hoping for a reply. When he has received this reply (probably the second character nods, or maybe brandishes the Jabberwock's head), he goes on to recommend another action.

This third kind of grammatical meaning — the kind which provides information about immediate situation, particularly about a speaker's or writer's intention towards his hearer or reader and the speaker's or writer's expectation from his hearer or reader — is called **interpersonal meaning**.

6.2.4 *Textual Meaning*

There is a fourth component of meaning which is called the **textual component**.

The textual component has two main functions.

Firstly it can be said that it is the textual component of meaning which makes any stretch of spoken or written language into a coherent and unified text rather than a set of miscellaneous sentences. For instance, if we compare the two sets of sentences,

A. *John saw a handbag in a field. John walked across a field and picked up a handbag. John took a handbag to the Police Station and John handed in a handbag as lost property. When John had handed in a handbag as lost property, John went home.*

B. *John saw a handbag in a field. He walked across the field and picked up the handbag. He took the handbag to the Police Station and handed it in as lost property. When he had done this, he went home.*

we find that the second set of sentences reads much more like a coherent and unified text than the first set. The two sets are exactly alike in their experiential, logical and interpersonal components. They differ only in their textual component. The first set of sentences ignores the fact that certain items recur and treats each occurrence of each item as if it were the first occurrence of the item. The second set of sentences uses the definite article *the* instead of the indefinite article *a* with some nouns which have occurred previously, substitutes the pronouns *he* and *it* for some other previously mentioned nouns, and substitutes the phrase *done this* for the second occurrence of *handed in a handbag as lost property*. It is these pronouns and other links between sentences that bind the sentences together and make them into a unified and coherent text. Binding devices such as these are known collectively as the **cohesion** of a text.

Jabberwocky can in some respects be said to be lacking in cohesion. Although it is in most respects a unified and coherent text, it does break some of the 'rules' of cohesion. For instance a pronoun is usually used, at any rate in formal written language, only in circumstances where it will be unambiguous. Either the thesis situation contains only one element to which the pronoun could conceivably refer, or the surrounding text disambiguates the pronoun by positioning the pronoun's antecedent noun fairly close to the pronoun and by assigning the antecedent noun to the same element of structure as the pronoun. (For example, in the second set of sentences cited above, the first *he* quite unambiguously refers to its antecedent noun *John,* since it occurs in the adjacent sentence to *John* and since it, like *John*, is acting as the subject of its clause. The later *hes* are also acting as the subjects of their clauses. Although these later *hes* are not very close to *John*, they are kept in touch with *John* by the intervening *hes*.) When the pronoun *he* is used in *Jabberwocky* it is by no means unambiguous. The situation does not make it clear who is meant by *he*; there are two characters in the story and the pronoun could refer to either. Nor does the immediately surrounding text disambiguate the pronoun. It is not at all clear what is the antecedent noun of the pronoun, or indeed if it has an antecedent noun. There is one noun which might be the antecedent − *son* in the first line of the second stanza − but this is four lines back even from the first occurrence of *he,* is used by a different speaker, and cannot really be said to be acting as the same element of structure as the pronoun. (As was explained in an earlier chapter, the 'subjects' of imperative clauses do not really count as subjects proper.) It seems likely that the last occurrence of *he* in the poem refers to the speaker of stanzas two and six, while all the other occurrences refer to the person addressed in stanzas two and six, but one only comes to this conclusion after a rather complicated process of reasoning and after reading the poem several times.

The second main function of the textual component is that of highlighting certain parts of the text. In Chapter 8 of Volume 1 the choice between marked theme and unmarked theme was discussed and in Chapter 4 of this volume mention was made of the choice between a marked position for the tonic and an unmarked position for the tonic. Both the choice of marked theme and the choice of a marked position for the tonic are ways of highlighting certain parts of a text. One example given of marked theme

Authority I respect, but authoritarianism I deplore

highlights *authority* and *authoritarianism.* Each of these items is acting as a complement. In each case the complement has been placed in front of its subject and predicator, a position which is comparatively unusual for it, and attention is drawn to it as a result. The example given in Chapter 4 of marked positioning of the tonic

// What shall / I / ask for? //

highlights *I.* Attention is drawn to *I* by the fact that it carries the tonic.

The first stanza of *Jabberwocky* has an example of marked theme:

All mimsy were the borogoves,

Here again the complement, *All mimsy,* has been placed in front of the subject and predicator, with the result that the quality it denotes is highlighted.

Often the highlighting function of the textual component is closely related to its cohesive function. The highlighting of *I* in

// What shall / I / ask for? //

implies that the speaker already knows what someone else is going to ask for. We can infer from this that, earlier in the text (the text in this case presumably being a conversation), somebody has indicated what someone else is going to ask for. The highlighting thus links the utterance

// What shall / I / ask for? //

with something that has occurred previously in the text. The highlighting shows that the utterance is just one bit of a whole unified text.

The choice of a marked position for the tonic always has a cohesive function in addition to its highlighting function. The choice of marked theme sometimes does.

More usually, however, the choice of marked theme has a purely highlighting function without the addition of a cohesive function. The *Jabberwocky* example of marked theme,

All mimsy were the borogoves,

cannot in any way be said to be linking its clause to what has gone before or what comes after. The marked theme simply draws special attention to the quality denoted by the complement. The function of the marked theme is a purely highlighting function.

As stated above, the experiential and logical components of the grammar are related to thesis situation, while the interpersonal component is related to immediate situation. It is less easy to state the relationship between the textual component and situation. In fact it is sometimes said that the textual component is wholly internal to language and has no relationship with anything extralinguistic at all. This, however, seems to be overstating the case. The textual component does seem to have some relationship with situation and therefore some sort of contextual meaning. It seems to have a relationship with both thesis and immediate situation. In fact it is the textual component which really provides the link between thesis and immediate situation by simultaneously having a relationship with both.

For instance, the pronoun *he,* in the second set of sentences about John and the handbag, has a relationship with an element of thesis 人 , just as the item *man* has. It also has a relationship with immediate situation: it indicates that the particular 人 in question has already been mentioned in the particular immediate situation. When someone uses the pronoun *he* in conversation, what he really means is 'I'm talking about a chap and the chap I'm talking about is the one who was referred to a little while ago in this same conversation.'

Similarly, the pronoun *I* in

// *What shall* | *I* | *ask for?* //

also links thesis and immediate situation. It, too, refers to an element of thesis 人 (or 人 !). It, too, has a relationship with immediate situation: it indicates that the particular 人 in question is actually present in the immediate situation and has adopted the role of speaker. Since in this example it is highlighted, *I* also has another relationship with immediate situation, a relationship which is an almost opposite kind of relationship to that described for *he* above. The highlighting indicates that the particular 人 in question is not the same one as has already been mentioned in the particular immediate situation. A speaker who highlights *I* in this way really means 'I'm talking about a chap, a chap who is actually here and speaking at the moment, and the chap I'm talking about is a different chap from the one who was referred to a little while ago in this conversation.'

When a speaker uses marked theme to highlight an item as in

Authority I respect,
All mimsy were the borogoves,

what he is really saying is 'You know from the experiential component of the meaning that the thesis situation includes a process involving two sets of participants. Well, the set of participants that I, the speaker in this immediate situation, want you, the hearer in this immediate situation, to take particular note of is the one I've placed in an unusual position.'

6.2.5 *Background Meaning*

As well as providing information about thesis, immediate situation and the connection between thesis and immediate situation, grammar can also provide information about wider situation.

If one speaker says *Do you want anything mending?* while another speaker says *Do you want anything mended?*, we can deduce that the two speakers come from different parts of the country. If one speaker says *You didn't ought to do that* while another speaker says *You ought not to do that,* we can deduce that the two speakers come from different social backgrounds.

The lack of cohesion noted in *Jabberwocky* is perhaps a grammatical clue to the fact that the poem stems from Looking-Glass Country, where everything is topsy-turvy and difficult to understand. (The lexis and graphology are certainly indicative of the poem's wider situation. Nothing could be more obscure than most of the lexical items. And the version of the poem which Alice sees is written in such a way that she has to hold it up to the mirror in order to read it.)

However, as in the case of lexis, the information provided by grammar about wider situation is more peripheral than the information about thesis and immediate situation. It cannot, therefore, be considered to be one of the fundamental components of the meaning in the way that the experiential, logical, interpersonal and textual are fundamental components.

It should be emphasised that the types of contextual meaning we have been discussing in Section 6.2 are not mutually exclusive. On the contrary

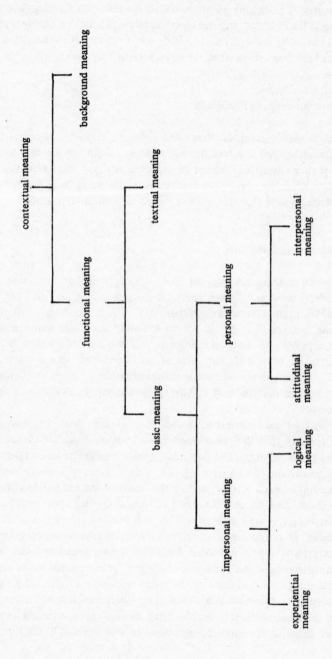

FIGURE 6.1

Types of contextual meaning

any given utterance will have experiential meaning *and* logical meaning *and* interpersonal meaning *and* textual meaning *and* background meaning.

6.3   A SUGGESTED WAY OF DIAGRAMMING THE DIFFERENT TYPES OF CONTEXTUAL MEANING TO SHOW HOW THEY ARE RELATED

At the bottom lefthand corner of Figure 6.1 comes experiential meaning. As we have seen, this is the component of the meaning of an utterance which provides information about the processes, participants and circumstances of each of the mini-situations which are being described.

Next to experiential meaning in the diagram comes logical meaning, which as we have seen is the component of the meaning which provides information about the way in which the mini-situations are related to form a maxi-situation.

Experiential meaning and logical meaning together provide the information about the thesis situation, about the situation which is being described. Jointly they form the component of the meaning of an utterance which is distinct from, apart from, the speaker. The speaker observes, selects and reports on the thesis situation but he does not otherwise intervene in this component of the meaning. This component of the meaning has nothing of the speaker himself in it. For this reason this component of the meaning has been called in the diagram *impersonal meaning.*

However the speaker adds to the impersonal ingredients of his message some personal ingredients making clear his own attitudes to the thesis and his own purpose in delivering his message.

As was implied in the last sentence the speaker's personal intervention in his message is of two kinds: information about the attitudes which he himself holds towards his thesis or ingredients of his thesis; and information about what he hopes to achieve by delivering his message.

The latter has already been exemplified in this chapter under the heading of *interpersonal meaning.*

The former can be exemplified by reference to the utterance *It must be raining.* The main ingredient of the thesis, of the impersonal meaning, of this utterance is the process of raining. The speaker has added to this impersonal ingredient a personal ingredient consisting of his own attitude towards the process, in this case his own assessment of the probability of the process taking place. The utterance *It must be raining* does not tell the hearer whether or not it actually is raining. It only tells him that the speaker thinks it is. Similarly we saw in Chapter 3 that the lexical item *cool,* as well as having an impersonal meaning relating to degree of temperature, could also have an attitudinal meaning relating to the speaker's assessment of the pleasantness or otherwise of this degree of temperature.

Impersonal meaning (experiential + logical meaning) and personal meaning (attitudinal + interpersonal meaning) have been grouped together in the diagram under the heading of *basic meaning.* These components of the meaning together provide the basic information of the message: information about the thesis, information about the speaker's attitudes, information about the speaker's purpose.

The speaker now intervenes in the message in a different way from the ways which were mentioned in the last few paragraphs. He now becomes the editor of his message. He has to consider the internal relationships of his message and the relative value as information of the various bits of his message. He has to ask himself such questions as How does this bit of my message relate to the earlier parts of my message? How many points do I want my hearer to get out of my message? Which ingredient do I want to come over as the most important? One of the impersonal ingredients? If so, which? Or one of the personal ingredients? If so, which? The speaker then arranges the cohesion of his utterance, the information distribution of his utterance, the information focus of his utterance, and the theme of his utterance, in such a way as to provide his hearer with information on the answers he has arrived at to the above questions. The speaker thus adds textual meaning to the basic meaning.

(Textual meaning is much more important than is sometimes realised. The actual form which a given utterance takes is often much more the direct result of its textual meaning than of the other components of its meaning.)

As we saw earlier in the chapter some information is communicated on purpose while other information is communicated unintentionally. All the kinds of information so far mentioned in this section are communicated on purpose. They are all purposeful, functional, kinds of meaning. Accordingly they have been grouped together in the diagram under the heading of *functional meaning.*

Information communicated unintentionally is represented in the diagram under the heading *background meaning.*

It should perhaps be pointed out that the term *interpersonal* is sometimes used to include the attitudinal component of meaning as well as the component of meaning which has been described as *interpersonal* in this chapter.

It should perhaps also be pointed out that background meaning could be subdivided into aspects relating to wider situation and aspects relating to immediate situation. Although there has not been room to illustrate them in this chapter, in addition to the aspects of immediate situation which give rise to functional meanings such as interpersonal meanings, there are also aspects of immediate situation which give rise to background meanings. Although they are not communicated on purpose, these aspects of immediate situation condition the form of language just as much as do the purposefully communicated aspects of immediate situation.

The functional kinds of meaning — experiential, logical, interpersonal and textual — are sometimes referred to in systemic linguistics as *functions*. This use of the term *function* has been avoided in this book as far as possible in order to prevent confusion with the other use of the term *function* as in Chapter 5, Section 5, of Volume 1. (See also page 6 of this volume.)

6.4 DISCUSSION

6.4.1 *General Linguistics*

The discussion section of the final chapter is perhaps a good place to summarise the main points of the systemic model of language:

Systemic linguistics sees language as a series of sets of contrasting options between which choices are made, these choices being primarily choices between different meanings.

The meanings between which choices are made are seen as potentialities for conveying certain information, these potentialities resulting from relationships of regular association between linguistic items or patterns and certain situational features. The meanings can be divided into types on the basis of the different aspects of situation involved in the relationships.

The form of language is fully determined by the meaning. When a speaker chooses a meaning he chooses a package deal as it were, an element of situation together with its partner, the linguistic item or pattern associated with that element of situation.

The situational member of such a partnership is realised by, made manifest by, the linguistic member.

The processes of realisation which lead from the situation of language to the form of language are seen as occurring in a number of stages: the inclusion, discontinuity, conflation, insertion, concatenation and particularisation processes of grammar; the particularisation processes of lexis; and insertion, concatenation and particularisation processes of phonology and/

or graphology.

Each meaning choice specifies only one move on the scale of realisation. It is a combination of meaning choices that leads to the complete form of a stretch of language.

At each of the formal levels of language, grammar, lexis, phonology and to a certain extent graphology, there are formal items. These formal items enter into the patterns and contrasts of their respective levels, the patterns and contrasts making it possible for the items to play their parts in the realisation processes listed above. In some cases the formal items enter into the patterns and contrasts as members of classes, in some cases as unique items.

At each of the formal levels the formal items are of differing size or status and can be related to each other on a scale of rank. The patterns and contrasts into which the items enter are similarly of differing status.

> As well as the contrasts which operate at each rank of unit, there are also in some cases contrasts between units. Decisions about which rank of item to assign to a particular amount of information – e.g. whether a particular amount of information should be assigned a sentence, a clause, or a group – provide an important part of the textual meaning of language.

Systemic linguistics is interested in all the above aspects of language both from the point of view of language potential and from the point of view of actual language. It is interested, that is, both in what people 'can say' in order to realise what they 'can mean' in relation to certain types of situation, and also in what a particular person 'does say' in order to realise what he 'does mean' in an actual situation.

> The above summary of the systemic model of language was written mainly with language potential in mind. If it were to be rewritten with actual language in mind, one or two modifications would be made. For instance in relation to language potential, meaning was said to be a potentiality for conveying information. In an actual utterance meaning would be the information actually conveyed.

Systemic linguistics is interested in relating language potential and actual language to each other. It is interested in considering what a particular person 'does say' in order to realise what he 'does mean' in an actual situation, in the light of the other things that he 'could have said' in order to realise the other things that he 'could have meant' in the type of situation of which the actual situation is an instance. It is also interested in observing what a particular person 'does say' in order to realise what he 'does mean' in an actual situation, with a view to testing its hypotheses about what people 'can say' in order to realise what they 'can mean' in that type of situation.

It should be emphasised that systemic linguistics is interested in situation types as well as in individual instances of situations, that systemic linguistics is interested in situation in relation to language potential as well as in relation to actual language. It is sometimes thought that situation is irrelevant to language potential, to *langue,* belonging only to actual language, to *parole.* Systemic linguistics regards the relationships between linguistic items and patterns and the various aspects of situation as an important part of language potential.

As has been indicated in this book, there are differences of opinion within the systemic school of linguistics. Not all systemic linguists would agree with all the details of the above summary of the systemic model.

One matter which is controversial, which indeed could at the moment be said to be *sub judice,* is particularly relevant to this chapter. This is the question of exactly where one draws the line between context and the formal levels of language.

In Chapter 2 context and system were shown as two separate points on the realisation scale, system being part of grammar. This formulation was adopted since systemicists usually have seemed to talk about context and system as if they were two separate categories and usually. have assigned system to grammar, although the grounds for distinguishing between them and for the positioning of system in grammar have not usually been made fully explicit.

However it could be argued, and this is the present view of the writer of this book, that context and system are one and the same point on the scale of realisation, system networks being simply cod-ifications of the contextual relationships discussed in this chapter.

The context-situation end of the realisation scale is an area of systemic grammar which still needs, and is at present receiving, a great deal more discussion.

6.4.2 *Descriptive Linguistics*

When we decide to describe a particular language or a particular variety of a language, rather than to discuss language in general, what we are really doing is to limit the range of the situation in which we are interested.

If we are discussing language in general, then the range of situation in which we are interested is limitless; everything in the universe and all aspects of everything in the universe are included.

If we decide to describe a particular language, then for the purposes of our study we set a limit on the range of situation. When we decide to describe a particular language it is really the wider situation whose range we are limiting, though we may also in the process be limiting the range of possible types of immediate situation.

If we decide to describe a particular regional, social or age dialect, we similarly limit the range of the wider situation and in so doing limit the range of possible types of immediate situation. But in this case the range is narrower than in the case of a whole language. In the case of a whole language we limit the range of the wider situation to that of the culture of the community who speak that language and we limit the range of the immediate situation to the types of immediate situation which occur within the framework of that culture. In the case of a dialect we limit the range of the wider situation to that of the sub-culture of the sub-community who speak that dialect and we limit the range of the immediate situation to the types of immediate situation which occur within the framework of that sub-culture.

If we decide to describe a particular register, we are limiting the range of the immediate situation. We are in fact limiting it to that of one particular type of immediate situation.

In each case, having limited the range of types of situation, we then try to discover firstly what functional meanings are possible in the given range of types of situation and secondly how these meanings are realised.

When we are describing a whole language, or a dialect, or a register, or even an idiolect, we are interested in language potential. We are interested in what meanings are possible in a given range of types of situation.

When we are considering a particular utterance, we are interested in actual language. We are interested in what meanings have actually been chosen in an actual situation.

However, as has been said, we usually consider actual language in the light of language potential. We consider the meanings actually chosen in the light of the meanings that could have been chosen. This means that we also need to consider the actual situation in the light of situation potential. We need to consider the actual situation as an instance of a type, or a range of types, of situation. A particular utterance is an instance of the realisation of a combination of meanings chosen from among the various meanings possible in the type of situation, or range of types of situation, of which the actual situation of the utterance is an instance.

The range of types of situation relevant to a particular utterance will depend on the form of language of which the utterance is being regarded as an instance. The same utterance could for the purposes of one study be regarded as an instance of a dialect, for the purposes of another study be regarded as an instance of a whole language. In the former case it would be the range of types of situation appropriate to the dialect that would be relevant, in the latter case the range of types of situation appropriate to the whole language.

6.4.3 *Contrastive Linguistics*

In a contrastive study of two languages, or varieties of a language, one works with three different ranges of types of situation. There is a range of types of situation appropriate to language (or variety of language) A and a range of types of situation appropriate to language (or variety of language) B. There is also a third range of types of situation.

Two things can be more effectively compared and contrasted if they are compared and contrasted within a common framework. Two forms of language can be more effectively compared and contrasted if they are both seen as instances of a more general form of language. If the Devonshire dialect and the Yorkshire dialect are being contrasted, they can be contrasted as varieties of English. If the language of *The Times* and the language of The *Daily Mirror* are being contrasted, they can be contrasted as sub-registers of the register of newspaper English. The range of types of situation appropriate to the more general form of language is relevant to the study as well as the ranges of types of situation appropriate to the forms of language actually being contrasted.

Having delimited the relevant ranges of types of situation, a contrastive study will then try to answer such questions as the following: which of the types of situation relevant to the more general form of language are relevant to form of language A, which to form of language B; which of the functional meanings possible in the more general form of language are possible in A, which in B; what is the frequency with which each of these meanings is chosen in A, what is the frequency in B; how are these meanings realised in A, how are they realised in B.

6.4.4 *Applied Linguistics*

For an applied linguistics study it is again a question of deciding on the limits of the situation in which one is interested.

Socio-linguistic studies, for instance, tend to limit the wider situation to that of a sub-culture, such as that of a particular socio-economic group (or if contrastive to the sub-cultures of two socio-economic groups). They tend to limit the immediate situation to that of a particular type of immediate situation, such as that of mother talking to child. They tend to limit the functional meaning in which they are interested to that of a particular type or sub-type of functional meaning. Sociolinguists have in fact shown particular interest in the meanings of the language of control, which is a sub-type of the interpersonal type of meaning. (It is not surprising that socio-linguists should show interest in a sub-type of the interpersonal type of meaning since of the various types of functional meaning, interpersonal meaning can perhaps be said to be the most social type of meaning.)

Examples of such studies can be found in Bernstein 1971 and 1972.

For literary studies, John Sinclair has pointed out that it is necessary to take into account two or even three sets of wider and immediate situation.[1]

If we were trying to explain the form of a line from *Macbeth*, for example, we should be able to do this partly on the basis of the inner situation of the play; on the basis, that is, of the wider situation of the character speaking as delimited by the play, on the basis of the type of immediate situation within the play in which the line is uttered, on the basis of the functional meanings being communicated.

However we should not be able to explain all aspects of the form in this way. For an explanation of some aspects of the form we should have to look to the situation of composition, to Shakespeare's own wider situation and to the type of immediate situation in which he wrote the play, that of a poet and a dramatist writing for an audience.

For an explanation of some other aspects of the form, such as the intonation patterns, we should have to look to a third kind of situation, the situation of performance, to the wider situation of the producer and the actors of a given production and to the immediate situation of a given performance.

Ruqaiya Hasan has pointed out that a distinctive characteristic of literary works is that they create their own situation;[2] create, that is, what John Sinclair has called their inner situation.

6.4.5 *Systemic Linguistics and Other Schools of Linguistics*

Systemic linguistics is more interested than other schools of linguistics in the aspects of situation other than thesis. Most other schools of linguistics have tended to confine their accounts of meaning to discussions of the relationships between linguistic items and elements of the thesis situation.

---

[1] In a talk to the Hull Linguistic Circle, February 1963.

[2] In a talk at University College, London, June 1968.

Systemic linguistics considers that if we are to be able to make any useful observations about the sociological aspects of language the other aspects of situation must be taken into account. It also considers that these other aspects of situation must be taken into account if we are satisfactorily to account for the form of language.

In particular it could be said that systemic linguistics has made a notable contribution to the study of textual meaning, a type of meaning neglected by other schools (though here acknowledgement must be made of the debt of systemic linguists to certain continental linguists, e.g. Firbas 1964, Vachek 1966).

The above remarks about the lack of interest of other schools in aspects of situation other than thesis are perhaps a little less true now than they were a few years ago. However the fact remains that what systemic linguistics has consistently stood for, perhaps more than anything else, from the days of Firthian linguistics, through scale-and-category linguistics, right up to the most recent form of systemic linguistics itself, is an interest in the relationships between language and the various aspects of the situation in which language is used.

Bibliography

CHAPTER 1

BERNSTEIN, B. (ed.) (1972) *Class, Codes and Control*, Vol. 2, London: Routledge & Kegan Paul

CATFORD, J. C. (1965) *A Linguistic Theory of Translation*, London: Oxford University Press

DOUGHTY, P. S., PEARCE, J. and THORNTON, G. (1971) *Language in Use*, London: Arnold

ELLIS, J. (1966) 'On contextual meaning' in Bazell, C. E., Catford, J. C., Halliday, M. A. K. and Robins, R. H. (eds.), *In Memory of J. R. Firth*, London: Longman

FIRTH, J. R. (1957) *Papers in Linguistics, 1934-1951*, London: Oxford University Press

HALLIDAY, M. A. K. (1961) 'Categories of the theory of grammar', *Word*, xvii, 241-92

– (1966) 'Some notes on "deep" grammar', *Journal of Linguistics*, ii, 57-67

– (1967a) *Some Aspects of the Thematic Organisation of the English Clause*, Santa Monica, California: The Rand Corporation

– (1967b) 'Notes on transitivity and theme in English', Part I, *Journal of Linguistics*, iii, 37-81; (1967c) Part II, *Journal of Linguistics*, iii, 199-244 and (1968) Part III, *Journal of Linguistics*, iv, 179-215

– (1969) 'Relevant models of language' in *The State of Language* (*Educational Review*, xxii, 26-37. University of Birmingham School of Education). Reprinted in Halliday (1973). See below

– (1970a) 'Language structure and language function' in Lyons, J. (ed.), *New Horizons in Linguistics*, Harmondsworth: Penguin Books

– (1970b) 'Functional diversity in language as seen from a consideration of modality and mood in English', *Foundations of Language*, vi, 322-61

– (1971a) 'Language in a social perspective' in *The Context of Language* (*Educational Review*, xxiii, 165-88, University of Birmingham School of Education). Reprinted in Halliday (1973). See below

– (1971b) 'Linguistic function and literary style: an inquiry into the language of William Golding's *The Inheritors*' in Chatman, S. (ed.), *The Proceedings of the Second Style in Language Conference (Bellagio, 1969)*, London: Oxford University Press. Reprinted in Halliday (1973). See below

– , McINTOSH, A. and STREVENS, P. D. (1964) *The Linguistic Sciences and Language Teaching*. London: Longman

HUDDLESTON, R. D. (1965) 'Rank and depth', *Language*, xli, 574-86
HUDSON, R. A. (1971) *English Complex Sentences*, Amsterdam: North-Holland
MUIR, J. (1972) *A Modern Approach to English Grammar*, London: Batsford
SINCLAIR, J. McH. (1965) *A Course in Spoken English, 3: Grammar*, prepub. edn and (1972) rev. edn, London: Oxford University Press

The above is a selection of the items listed in the bibliographies of Volume 1. For readers interested in the development of Systemic Linguistics the following are recommended: Firth 1957; Halliday 1961; Halliday, McIntosh and Strevens 1964; Huddleston 1965; Ellis 1966; Halliday 1966; Halliday 1967b and c and Halliday 1968; Halliday 1970a; Halliday 1970b; Halliday 1971a; Hudson 1971. For readers interested in systemic descriptions of English the following are recommended: Halliday 1967a; Halliday 1967b and c and Halliday 1968; Halliday 1970b; Hudson 1971; Muir 1972; Sinclair 1965 and 1972. An impression of some of the applications of Systemic Linguistics can be obtained from: Bernstein 1972; Catford 1965; Doughty, Pearce and Thornton 1971; Halliday 1969; Halliday 1971b.

Works which have become available since most of this book was written include the following:

FAWCETT, R. P. (1973a) *Systemic Functional Grammar in a Cognitive Model of Language*, University College, London: mimeographed
– (1973b) *Generating a Sentence in Systemic Functional Grammar*, University College, London: mimeographed
– (1974) 'Some proposals for systemic syntax' Part I, in *MALS* (Midlands Association for Linguistic Studies) *Journal*, i
– (1975) 'Summary of "Some issues concerning levels in systemic models of language" ', *Nottingham Linguistic Circular*, iv
– (Forthcoming) 'Two concepts of function in a cognitive model of communication' in Candlin, C. N. (ed.), *The Communicative Teaching of English*, London: Longman
HALLIDAY, M. A. K. (1973) *Explorations in the Functions of Language*, London: Arnold
– (1974a) *Language and Social Man*, London: Longman (Schools Council Programme in Linguistics and English Teaching, Papers, Series II, 3)
– (1974b) 'Language as social semiotic', in Makkai, Adam and Makkai, V. B. (eds.), *The First LACUS Forum*, Columbia, S. Carolina: Hornbeam Press
– (1975) *Learning How to Mean*, London: Arnold
– (Forthcoming) 'Text as semantic choice in social contexts', in Van Dijk, T. A. and Petofi, J. S. (eds.), *Grammars and Descriptions*, Berlin and New York: De Gruyter
– (Forthcoming) *The Meaning of Modern English*, London: Oxford University Press (referred to in Volume 1 of this book as *An Outlook on Modern English*)
– and HASAN, Ruqaiya (1976) *Cohesion in English*, London: Longman

HUDSON, R. A. (1974) 'Systemic generative grammar', *Linguistics*, cxxxix
— (1975) 'The meaning of questions', *Language*, li
KRESS, Gunther (ed.) (Forthcoming) *System and Function in Language*, London: Oxford University Press
SINCLAIR, J. McH. and JONES, S. (1974) 'English lexical collocations', *Cahiers de Lexicologie*, xxiv
WINOGRAD, T. (1972) *Understanding Natural Language*, Edinburgh: The University Press

CHAPTER 2

HALLIDAY, M. A. K. (1961) 'Categories of the theory of grammar', *Word*, xvii, 241-92
— (1969) 'Options and functions in the English clause', *Brno Studies in English*, viii, 81-88. Reprinted in Householder, F. W. (ed.) (1972) *Syntactic Theory I: Structuralist*, Harmondsworth: Penguin Books
— (1971) 'Language in a social perspective', in *The Context of Language* (*Educational Review*, xxiii, 165-188, University of Birmingham School of Education.) Reprinted in Halliday, M. A. K. (1973) *Explorations in the Functions of Language*, London: Arnold
HUDSON, R. A. (1971) *English Complex Sentences*, Amsterdam: North-Holland
TURNER, G. J. (1972) 'Social class and children's language of control at age 5 and age 7', in Bernstein, B. (ed.) *Class, Codes and Control*, Vol. 2, London: Routledge & Kegan Paul

The main sources for this chapter are the above-listed works together with a talk given by Professor Halliday to the Nottingham Linguistic Circle in May 1967 and the typescript of a talk given by Professor Halliday in Rome in May 1967.

For a more detailed account of some of the processes of realisation readers are recommended to see Hudson 1971. For a socio-linguistic study making use of the concept of realisation, Turner 1972 is recommended.

CHAPTER 3

HALLIDAY, M. A. K. (1961) 'Categories of the theory of grammar', *Word*, xvii, 241-92
— (1966) 'Lexis as a linguistic level' in Bazell, C. E., Catford, J. C., Halliday, M. A. K. and Robins, R. H. (eds.) *In Memory of J. R. Firth*, London: Longman
SINCLAIR, J. McH. (1966) 'Beginning the study of lexis' in Bazell, C. E., Catford, J. C., Halliday, M. A. K. and Robins, R. H. (eds.) *In Memory of J. R. Firth*, London: Longman
— , JONES, S. and DALEY, R. (1970) *English Lexical Studies*, Birmingham University: mimeographed

The main sources for this chapter are the above-listed works together with talks given by Professor J. McH. Sinclair to the Linguistics Association of Great Britain and to various groups at the University of Nottingham.

Halliday 1966 is particularly recommended as a theoretical discussion of the relations between lexis and grammar, Sinclair et al. 1970 as a practical lexical study.

CHAPTER 4

ABERCROMBIE, D. (1964) 'A phonetician's view of verse structure' in Abercrombie, D. (1965), *Studies in Phonetics and Linguistics*, London: Oxford University Press

ALBROW, K. H. (1968) *The Rhythm and Intonation of Spoken English* (Paper 9. *Programme in Linguistics and English Teaching*), London: Longman

HALLIDAY, M. A. K. (1967a) *Intonation and Grammar in British English*, The Hague: Mouton

– (1967b) 'Notes on transitivity and theme in English', Part II, *Journal of Linguistics*, iii, 199-244; (1968) Part III, *Journal of Linguistics*, iv, 179-215

– (1970) *A Course in Spoken English: Intonation*, London: Oxford University Press

The above-listed works have acted as the sources for this chapter and are recommended for further study. Halliday 1970 is available on tape.

CHAPTER 5

ABERCROMBIE, D. (1951) 'R.P. and local accent' in Abercrombie, D. (1965), *Studies in Phonetics and Linguistics*, London: Oxford University Press

– (1963) 'Conversation and spoken prose', in Abercrombie, D. (1965). See above

– (1964) 'A phonetician's view of verse structure' in Abercrombie, D. (1965). See above

ALBROW, K. H. (1970) *The English Writing System: Notes towards a Description*, University College, London: mimeographed

HALLIDAY, M. A. K. (1961) 'Categories of the theory of grammar', *Word*, xvii, 241-92

– , McINTOSH, A. and STREVENS, P. D. (1964) *The Linguistic Sciences and Language Teaching*, London: Longman

MACKAY, D. and THOMPSON, B. (1968) *The Initial Teaching of Reading and Writing* (Paper 3. *Programme in Linguistics and English Teaching*), London: Longman

McINTOSH, A. (1961) ' "Graphology" and meaning' in McIntosh, A. and Halliday, M. A. K. (1966), *Patterns of Language*, London: Longman

The main sources for this chapter are Halliday 1961 and Halliday et al. 1964.

McIntosh 1961 is recommended for further reading on theoretical issues. Albrow 1970 (now published as Volume 2 of *The Schools Council*

Programme in Linguistics and English Teaching: Papers, Series II, London: Longman) is a descriptive study of English graphology. Abercrombie 1951 and Abercrombie 1963 are relevant respectively to a contrastive study of regional varieties of English and a contrastive study of spoken registers of English. Abercrombie 1964 is very highly recommended for its approach to English prosody and Mackay and Thompson 1968 for its approach to the teaching of reading and writing.

CHAPTER 6

BERNSTEIN, B. (ed.) (1971) *Class, Codes and Control,* Vol. 1; (1972) *Class, Codes and Control,* Vol. 2, London: Routledge & Kegan Paul

ELLIS, J. (1966) 'On contextual meaning' in Bazell, C. E., Catford, J. C., Halliday, M. A. K. and Robins, R. H. (eds.) *In Memory of J. R. Firth,* London: Longman

FIRBAS, J. (1964) 'On defining the theme in Functional Sentence Analysis', *Travaux linguistiques de Prague,* i, 267-80

FIRTH, J. R. (1957) 'Modes of meaning', in Firth, J. R., *Papers in Linguistics, 1934-1951,* London: Oxford University Press

GREGORY, M. (1967) 'Aspects of varieties differentiation', *Journal of Linguistics,* iii, 177-98

HALLIDAY, M. A. K. (1961) 'Categories of the theory of grammar', *Word,* xvii, 241-92

— (1969) 'Options and functions in the English clause', *Brno Studies in English,* viii, 81-88. Reprinted in Householder, F. W. (ed.) (1972) *Syntactic Theory I: Structuralist,* Harmondsworth: Penguin Books

— (1970) 'Language structure and language function', in Lyons, J. (ed.) *New Horizons in Linguistics,* Harmondsworth: Penguin Books

— (1971) 'Language in a social perspective' in *The Context of Language* (*Educational Review,* xxiii, 165-88. University of Birmingham School of Education). Reprinted in Halliday, M. A. K. (1973) *Explorations in the Functions of Language,* London: Arnold

— , McINTOSH, A. and STREVENS, P. D. (1964) *The Linguistic Sciences and Language Teaching,* London: Longman

HASAN, R. (1968) *Grammatical Cohesion in Spoken and Written English, I* (Paper 7 of *Programme in Linguistics and English Teaching*), London: Longman

TURNER, G. J. (1972) 'Social class and children's language of control at age 5 and age 7', in Bernstein (1972). See above

VACHEK, J. (1966) *The Linguistic School of Prague,* Bloomington, Ind.; London: Indiana University Press

The main sources for this chapter are Ellis 1966, Firth 1957, Halliday 1961, 1969, 1970 and 1971, Halliday et al. 1964 and Turner 1972. These are recommended for further reading together with Gregory 1967 which is relevant to contrastive studies of different registers.

Index

Bold face numbers indicate the passage where the explanation of a technical term is to be found. References in square brackets are to Volume 1.